PURE WISDOM

PURE WISDOM

*Insights for those Seeking Happiness
and Peace of Mind*

---

by
SHANTANAND SARASWATI

ALLWON
PUBLISHING CO

ALLWON
PUBLISHING CO.

3000 Redhill Avenue
Costa Mesa, CA 92626

Library of Congress Cataloging-in-Publication Data

Shantanand Saraswati, Swami, 1946-
       Pure wisdom: insights for those seeking happiness and peace of mind / by Shantanand Saraswati.
          p. cm.
       Includes index.
       ISBN 1-880741-24-5 (pbk. : alk. paper)
       1. Spiritual life.   I. Title.
       BL624.S477 1992
       291.4 4—dc20   91-77864
                                                       CIP

Book and cover design by Beth Hansen
Cover photograph by Tom Fridmann
Edited by Naomi Rose
Desktop production by Janet Andrews

Printed on acid free paper

10   9   8   7   6   5   4   3   2   1   0

To
All those Seekers
of
Truth and Freedom

TABLE
OF
CONTENTS

IF YOU
COULD HAVE
ANYTHING . . .

IF GOD CAME into your life in person and asked you, "What would you like to have?," what would you ask from God? "You may have one thing or as many things as you want," He tells you, but adds, "There is one condition: As the price for whatever you ask, I will take away from your life one thing. What would you like to ask in exchange for just one thing?" Of course, God is being clever and not telling you what that one thing is.

Then God tells you, "I will grant your desires, I will give you the best health, the most money, the most beautiful gardens, palaces, and lovers—but I will take away your capacity to feel love."

Would you be willing to make such a bargain?

Somehow you know that without the capacity to experience love, you would not be able to enjoy anything. You would feel like an alien, unable to communicate. No matter what we have or don't have in life, the most important thing is the capacity to experience love. You may think you are not worthy of being loved or not capable of expressing love, but as long as you have this capacity to experience love, you need not be concerned whether you are worthy. It is

1

more than enough just to appreciate the simple gift of being able to experience love.

———————————

THE
MYSTIC
WITHIN

WHETHER YOU are loved or expressing love, there is something mystical about appreciating this gift of love and allowing the flower of love to blossom in your heart. You feel love toward children, flowers, birds, the ocean, and so on. Celebrate that and recognize how blessed you are to feel that sort of energy, connection, and oneness. When you recognize that gift in you without wondering whether it is enough or not enough, pure or not pure, you are blessed with it, and it becomes a mystical experience. You are not only alive, you feel love. If you don't know what you did to experience this love, to deserve it, then it is a gift. Somehow in the scheme of life you got it. Be grateful.

When you let your mind become saturated with the gratitude of your heart, you find this love becomes more and more intense, more and more overwhelming. It becomes so intense and overwhelming that you find your separate, ego-based identity losing itself in that fountain of love, in that wellspring of gratitude. It is sweet, as if you put a sugar cube in water and that sugar cube just melts and melts. Your mind melts, and the more you recognize this process, the more your recognition and awareness help the process.

It is because of your thoughts about the past and future that you feel fragmented. All spiritual disciplines are meant to give you an experience of wholeness and show you how to become whole. The more you become whole, the more you appreciate wholeness and start merging in this wholeness. In the end, you realize that you were never anything but wholeness. When one of us realizes that he or she is nothing but wholeness, then we call that person an extraordinary person, a mystic. We have a mystic sleeping within each of us. You can know it by knowing you have this gift, this capacity of experiencing love. You don't have to do anything; it is just there. When you recognize and appreciate it, it blossoms and blasts its container. When the container is blasted, you are no longer there; only love is there.

Stop Judging
The Flow of Life

BECAUSE OF misunderstandings, you are cruel to yourself more than to others. If you were cruel only toward others it wouldn't hurt so much, but you become cruel to others by first becoming cruel to yourself. You become cruel by being overly judgmental about the flow of life that is expressing through you and through the other person. If you don't like yourself, how can you like anyone else? How can you even like God?

If you could like yourself, then wherever you went you would find others liking you, and you would start liking them. If you dislike yourself, you project that they don't like you. Then you have resentment toward them. If they don't like you, how will you be able to like them? You are not able to recognize that it is you inspiring them to like or not like you. They are simply following your subtle suggestions.

How can you love yourself? You can love yourself by leading a simple, regulated life based on common sense. You can love yourself by remembering your focal point, the symbol of your Divine being. You can love yourself by taking good care of your health and creativity. When you really love and accept yourself, then automatically you transcend yourself. When you transcend yourself, you lose yourself—but you don't really lose anything: You become the vast Self. In that Self, no one is separate from you. You need nobody's love and recognition; it is all you. Can you complain to anyone when your own teeth bite your tongue? Teeth and tongue are not separate from you. How can we reach that mystical high that is hidden within us?

In our Indian mythology, we are given a beautiful story about our creation. By nature, God was addicted to meditating and being blissed out. One day, instead of just being blissed out in meditation, He felt like being playful. In that playfulness, He visualized, "Let me be many and enjoy myself through many colorful names and forms." According to this story, we all came into being because of that Divine fantasy. Since we are the Divine expression, and since we came into existence because of that Divine playfulness, we cannot be content just meditating and being blissed out. There is something within us that craves to be playful, loving, and friendly. If we trust in God and in His playfulness, we should express this side of our being; and the more we express this side of our being, the more we are loyal to God and the more we feel a sense of wholeness, love, and oneness with each and every one who comes into our life.

FINDING WAYS
TO LOVE

I FIND SOME people very self-centered. They are not less
kind, but they just want to be left alone. When I go for
walks, I seldom find anyone walking; if someone is walking,
he is just walking by himself, seldom with his spouse or a
friend; if he is walking with his spouse or friend, he does
not care to talk to strangers.

There is something good and great about not having
abundance —you learn to depend on others. You learn to
trust others with a humble attitude: "Could you do me a
favor? Otherwise I'm stuck." Since you have also been
stuck sometimes, you have that understanding, you know
that's how life works, so you reach out without being
egotistical. In that sort of interaction, you learn to be playful
and loving, and unknowingly you develop a sense of friendliness.

In the West, it is so formal. If you go to a lecture, you
pay a certain price; if you go to a counselor, you pay a
certain fee. It is always a business relationship. Business is
business; it is not love and friendliness. You may seem to
interact with hundreds of people in your business, but you
do not truly interact with a single person.

CREATE A SPACE
FOR LOVE

IF YOU CAN afford it, spend twenty dollars every month just for inviting friends over. Please don't invite them to a restaurant. Invite them to your home, and try to cook with your own hands. Don't worry whether others will like your cooking or not; that is not the point. Let them feel you care for their company, their support, their cheerfulness. You will start feeling wonderful about yourself. It is something that just happens. Logic cannot explain such things. When you fall in love with someone, it is an experience. So when you open your heart with the attitude of friendliness and really make friends, life becomes more enjoyable.

I am blessed to have so many friends across the country, but I don't feel I have enough. It is great to be mystical and transcend our physical limitations of body, mind and feelings, but there is something great in loving someone too. To experience love, you have to create a space for love, and creating that space for love means inviting certain persons into your heart and home. They all are going to be strangers in the beginning, so don't think you have to start with your friends. You can start with strangers or acquaintances. They will become friends.

Most of the time you are very concerned about comfort and money, but when you really love someone, you don't mind sharing your comfort and money to comfort that person. The person could be your child, your mother, father, brother, sister, lover, or anyone. Even though you are losing your time, money, and comfort, why don't you *feel* like a loser? Because you realize that it is more joyful to have that person be well than to have any amount of time, money, or comfort.

INVESTING
IN
LOVE

How do you develop that sort of love? You start by taking an interest and sharing something you have in your life. There is something in your investment of time, energy, and money that makes you emotionally involved with a person, and you cannot remain aloof, you feel love for that person. If you invest your time, energy, and money in an organization, you cannot remain unconcerned about the progress of that organization.

You become emotionally involved. Why don't we invest more? Because we don't know whether a person or place is going to bring us good dividends. We don't want to plant seeds because we may lose the seeds and never get the plants. So we hold onto what we have gained through our sacrifices.

In my childhood, I heard a story about a sage. There was a battle going on between demons and gods, and the gods were being defeated by the demons. Indra, the king of the gods, was advised that if he made a special weapon with the bones of a holy man, Dadhichi, he would be able to kill his enemies.

Indra wondered, "Who could be such a holy man that

he would willingly give up his body for our safety and victory?" When Indra went to Dadhichi, the sage said, "There could be no better use for this old body. I have lived enough. It is time for me to move on, and I was wondering what this body could be used for." Gently he closed his eyes, went into his final trance and died. With his bones the weapon was made, and the demons were defeated.

Although I don't imagine that you or I can reach such a height in this lifetime, it is inspiring to remember the ideal. It energizes us to live life with that goal of selfless service and celebration. Whatever you enjoy in life is not because of health, money, or any "thing." It is because you have this gift of love. Enhance this gift of love by being more kind, more tender, more loving, more friendly, more playful. When you make others feel loved, you automatically feel blessed and realize that the greatest miracle of life is to be happy by making someone else happy. Perhaps you are looking for miracles through exploring your kundalini, chakras, and visions. They are there, but they are secondary. You can experience the real juice of life, the nectar of life, through being happy by making someone else happy.

One of the best experiences I ever had was with a dog who I lived with some years ago. Now, by nature I am a very lazy person. If I hate anything about myself, it is my laziness. When I patted the dog, he would start wagging his tail. If I rubbed him a little more, he would lie down and roll over as though asking for more from me, and I would end up giving him a loving massage for five minutes. How could such a lazy person like me be persuaded to give a massage—and to a dog? Because the one who was receiving that massage knew how to receive it! The beauty was not in my giving; it was in his receiving. I used to give him a massage almost every day, because when I did I felt so filled with love, compassion, and joy that it was impossible for me not to. He knew the trick of how to receive.

When we open ourselves with that tenderness, gentleness, and humility, we help others to also open to the same wavelength, the same rapport, the same sensitivity. Then it is fun. There is no greater fun than to love someone, to see God in someone. What an awesome experience.

But we have to start somewhere.

WHAT'S
IN
THE BASKET?

VISUALIZE A tiny, sweet, cute child. Now realize that this visualization could be done with any one of us. We may not be sweet and cute in each other's eyes, but we all are very sweet and cute in the eyes of our Creator because we are His or Her children, and children are always sweet and cute in the eyes of their parents.

Imagine this child walking in a beautiful garden with a tiny, beautiful basket in her hand. Can you imagine it? In that huge garden she picks just one flower and puts that flower into her basket. She is thrilled. She knows that her basket cannot contain more than a flower, so she's content.

Now, you have a very small, cute basket. What is that basket? The basket is this moment. You are carrying this moment with you. It can contain only one, single flower, only one, single thought at a time. I haven't found anyone smart enough to think more than one thought in a moment. So here is your basket of the moment, and here is the sweet flower of your thought or feeling. Is it heavy? The problem arises when you think you have to squeeze *all* the flowers of the world, *all* the thoughts, *all* the fantasies into your tiny basket of the moment. It is very liberating to know that you have to carry only one sweet flower, since your basket cannot hold more than one at a time.

Your spiritual wisdom starts by becoming aware of this flower in your basket of the moment. You may consider it a huge responsibility, or you may consider it very easy and playful.

See what is happening in your life. You are carrying your basket, but you are neither aware of your basket nor of the flower in your basket. So you are in sweet inertia. You are here, there, and everywhere without knowing where you are and what your basket/moment is containing. You are either living in inertia or fighting with yourself, trying to squeeze in more flowers of the past and future. When you realize the hopelessness of it, you become liberated. God has given each of us the capacity to handle a single flower, a single thought, or a single feeling lovingly and wisely. When we become aware of our thoughts moment by moment, they don't bother us. You may find that sometimes you are not carrying any flower in the basket. The basket is empty. If you can be aware of this emptiness, you will experience a unique sense of freedom in that moment. Once you experience freedom, you exude that freedom wherever you are. You always exude what you are, whether you want to or not.

What is this flower, this thought, this feeling? Put your energy on it, zoom into it. Suppose you are not feeling great, you are feeling jealous, angry, or insecure. Be aware of it, feel it out, then see what you can do. If you can do something, do it, and you will feel blessed about yourself for doing it.

Suppose there is a dead mouse in your room. It does not smell like sweet roses, so you have to leave your seat and throw it away. While you are throwing it away, you are disgusted, but you feel great that you are not just praying,

"God, please take care of this problem so the mouse gets transported to heaven." You are not being lazy and asking someone else to do it. You have to do it. Your meditation is not yet strong enough to evaporate that mouse.

DO SOMETHING
OR
EXPERIENCE FULLY

EITHER DO something, or experience your feeling and let it saturate your being. The feeling is not going to kill you. It will be consumed by you. You have so much Divine power of peace, love, wisdom, and awareness that no sins in the whole world can tarnish the Divinity within you. The clouds may cover the sky, but they never rob the blueness from the sky. Clouds appear and disappear.

If you feel jealous, angry, or insecure, remember your focal point, your Divine symbol, as though you are experiencing this emotion through your focal point. To your great surprise, you will find that this tiny focal point has enough power to burn away all the impurities and negative feelings.

Either do something, or accept totally. The greatest rift you create in your psyche, which prevents you from being able to appreciate the flower in the moment, is that you seldom appreciate yourself for what you do or can do. You always think you could have or should have done better: "Oh, I'm all right, but ...." You have to wipe out this "but" and realize, "I am fine here and now." Unless you develop trust you cannot be really happy, you cannot feel a sense of wholeness. You think that unless you go to a temple or a teacher or read certain books, you are not going to experience bliss. Bliss is already within you. When you are having a nightmare, and someone awakens you, you feel saved, you feel grateful, but you were really saved all the time and didn't know it.

When we see life from that perspective, we see that life is just for play. God was having a good time in His blissful meditation. If He goofed, it is so that we could learn to be more playful. I really don't know why some people are so heavy and take themselves so seriously. What is so serious? Let us be more playful, loving, and grateful.

GRATITUDE

IN INDIA ONE time, I was begging from door to door and had taken a vow to not handle money or buy food. Although India is a very kind country, sometimes it is tough there too. One day, I was not offered anything to eat. I felt as though I were starving. When, ultimately, I got some food, I knew right away that the food was not fresh. I thanked God from the depths of my heart because I was nearly on the brink of starvation. I started eating with a thankful heart. Later, it dawned on me that if the same food had been offered to me by my sister, I would have thrown it away and scolded her. I realized that what makes us resentful or grateful is not a particular act or object but our attitude toward it. When you don't have this sense of "right" and expectation, your heart is filled with gratitude. If I am selfless and you smile at me once, it is more than enough to keep me grateful to you for life. But if I am selfish and you give me a million dollars, I may feel resentful for not having gotten more.

Once Buddha's disciple was going out into the world to preach, and Buddha asked, "Suppose others start ridiculing you. How will you react?"

The disciple said, "I will feel grateful to them because they are kind enough to merely ridicule me and not throw stones at me."

Then Buddha asked, "Suppose they start throwing stones at you?"

The disciple replied, "I will feel loved and accepted because at least they are not kicking me."

Then Buddha asked, "If someone starts kicking you, how will you feel?" The disciple said, "Still I will feel grateful because they are not killing me." Then Buddha asked, "If one of them starts killing you?" The disciple said, "I will tune into my inner light, lit by you, and remember your teaching that the Cosmic Scheme is releasing me from this garment of flesh and blessing me with *nirvana.*"

———————————

FORGIVENESS

TO FORGIVE others, you have to know how to forgive yourself. To forgive yourself, you have to know the whole spectrum of what makes you do what you do. Don't be too harsh and judgmental on yourself. We are like puppets in the Divine Scheme. When you realize it is just the flow of life manifesting through you, you become very accepting of yourself and others. When you care to know what is going on in someone's life, automatically you find a stream of love flowing toward that person.

ATTITUDE
AND
THE QUALITY OF LIFE

THE MORE WE understand about the importance of attitude, the more we understand how it determines the quality of life. When we have the attitude of being losers, life is not pleasant for us; but if we take on Jesus' meaning of loser—"Unless you lose yourself you will not find your Self"—our feelings change, and losing becomes a great achievement. "Yourself" means the ego and desiring mind. "Your Self" means that universal Self which is the background of the individual mind or ego.

If we investigate deeply, this mind or ego is struggling to realize the fullness and abundance that is beyond our human boundaries. No matter how hard the ego tries and no matter what it achieves, if it remains limited and separated from other beings, it will never have the satisfaction of that fullness. All our achievements ultimately are directed to make us lose ourselves.

GIVING
AND
RECEIVING

YOUR ATTITUDE swings between giving and receiving, and you are not sure which attitude to develop. It feels good to your ego to be a giver, giving gifts, compliments, time, energy, or money: You are more in control, you feel good about yourself, you are not dependent, you are making others comfortable and happy. But as a giver you feel you may lose something, and you don't want to lose. You don't know how to give without losing, so you never give wholeheartedly. You hold back because you don't want to be a sucker.

When you have the attitude of receiver, there is a certain loneliness; you feel inferior and not quite confident about yourself. You feel as if you are put down by others, and you don't like yourself for being on the receiving side. Receiving does not give good feedback to your ego. So at Christmas you like to give and take—to share.

THE ATTITUDE
OF
SELFLESS SHARING

SHARING FEELS better than giving or receiving. But there is an even higher perspective. If we go deeper, we realize that sharing still connotes a duality, a separation and boundaries. The real joy of life comes when we have an attitude of oneness or relatedness. Then we share without feeling a sense either of pride when we give or of loss when we receive. Sharing comes naturally. My hand puts food in the mouth, and there is a sense of oneness and relatedness. My hand doesn't feel superior, nor does my mouth feel inferior. They belong to the same body unit. Whether we share by giving or by receiving, it is through selfless sharing that we reach that higher dimension of oneness or relatedness. Until we reach that state of consciousness, we will remain a little up or a little down, and we have to accept that.

If we have a negative attitude toward a problem, we treat the problem as a big one and worry about how to get out of it. If we have a healthy and open attitude toward a problem, we take the problem as a sweet challenge that energizes us and reminds us of our basic potential. It puts us in a creative and dynamic space, shakes us up from our inertia and laziness, and makes us get in touch with our Divine potential. When we are open and willing to have a problem, we look at the same problem with a different attitude. When we have this attitude, a problem is not a problem.

ACCEPTANCE

THE FIRST attitude is acceptance.

If you had no problems, would you have learned what you have learned? Driving a car, working on computers, the existence of television or any other human invention—all were in some way the result of facing a problem with a healthy attitude. Someone faced it and in so doing improved the quality of life. When we are stuck with a problem, we don't enjoy the flow of life. So our first attitude should be to avoid viewing it as a problem, yet without denying that it is a problem.

You have to go to the bathroom every day; you have to brush your teeth; you have to get your hair cut. But these are not big problems. Because you are able to accept and accommodate these, they have become normal in the flow of life. When you are more evolved, more detached, and objective, you realize that every problem is merely a life situation that demands your attention and action. When you see every problem as a life situation, it fills your heart with courage and zeal.

If you have a puzzle box and keep rearranging the cubes, you don't curse the person who made the puzzle. You enjoy

25

doing it because you are detached. You know it doesn't matter whether you are able to solve it or not. When you feel you have to solve and resolve things, your ego comes into the picture. Instead, be open: "If I do it, fine. If I don't do it, also fine. There is something here to challenge my head and my heart; there is something here to challenge my dynamism and zeal." It is all a matter of attitude, and learning how to deal with a problem in a healthy way will be very rewarding throughout your entire life.

PROBLEMS
ARE SITUATIONS
FOR GROWTH

LIFE KEEPS moving and unfolding, and none of us can fix it. If life is fixed, there is no fun, no joy, no growth, no celebration. If you fix the course of the river and it is not flowing naturally, it is no longer a river—it is just a stagnant body of water. Every moment of life is unique and new. We don't know what will happen. So remain open to each new moment as a great lover and friend.

If you have been raised to believe in God, take advantage of that faith. Realize that you have been put in a particular life situation with your Divine mother or father to learn a special lesson, and move on in the unfoldment of your consciousness. God is not concerned with your having pleasant and superfluous experiences. God is concerned with your growth, so there really is no problem; the supposed problem is simply a stepping stone.

If you are going through the labor of childbirth, it is a painful time. You cannot deny the pain, but you trust that through this pain you will give birth to a wonderful child, a living flower who will enhance the glory of your womanhood as a mother. It is great to be a mother. Without mothers we couldn't be here. Because your attitude is positive, you are willing to go through the pain, and you accept that pain lovingly and joyfully.

If you can go through the toughest pain graciously, you can go through any life situation. There is glory in pain, but our negative attitude keeps us from seeing the beauty of it. With faith, your attitude is one of surrendering and accepting a problem as a situation for growth. You surrender your problems and yourself at the feet of the Lord and let Him inspire you about how to handle the problem without fighting or resisting it. You know the problem is for your growth, and even if you are going through pain you have a positive attitude. The more you develop this attitude of confidence about yourself and your ability to go through any life situation, the more you maintain a positive attitude of serenity. Through the attitude of surrendering you can handle a problem in a positive and detached way.

WATCHFULNESS

T HE SECOND attitude is watchfulness.
Suppose you don't feel inclined to trust in Cosmic
Providence or God. What can you do? Through an attitude
of watchfulness, you just watch the problem and see objectively how overwhelming the pain of the problem is.
Instead of going through the pain of a problem, mind
usually tries to ignore, deny, or fight with the problem to
get out of it. Instead, own the problem, lick it, beat it. When
you own and accept the problem, you are much more
powerful than any problem you are going through. All
problems arise in you and fizzle out in you. They may look
overwhelming in the beginning, but if you don't lose patience and poise and if you accept the storm of the problem,
you will find that although it is very overwhelming, it
cannot last.

In the process of going through a problem, you may feel
like having a drink, watching television, having sex, or
playing with your dog or cat. Indulge yourself objectively.
If so, ask yourself, "Am I really feeling the pain of the
problem right now, or am I feeling the pleasure of this
diversion?" If you are diverting yourself, you experience a

little relief from the pain.

Mind has developed the attitude, "Life is a problem; I'm going through the mill." Who is going through this mill? When you are more aware of the Essence that is the substratum of all your experiences, you will know that it makes no difference whether you go through hell or heaven. The fact is that we all go through pleasant and unpleasant experiences.

Whatever we energize with our attitude becomes overwhelming. We know that Gandhi was shot; Mother Teresa is not always enjoying television and having face lifts, yet she doesn't feel unhappy. She is so sweet, so humble and content, like a child. Even while Jesus was being crucified, he maintained his attitude of oneness: "Forgive them, Father, for they know not what they do." At a certain stage of consciousness, you develop an attitude of acceptance and openness, but that will come only when you don't deny your problems and fight with them.

A problem is simply a thought. The more you question yourself, "Do I have a problem or do I not have a problem?", the more you will find, "Right now, I don't have a problem." The more you are aware of these moments of problemlessness, the more you develop a positive attitude that life is just a flow of consciousness, an expression of Divine celebration. When you are ready for higher understanding and wisdom, that is the greatest transformation that you can go through.

DECISIVENESS

THE THIRD attitude is decisiveness.

No matter what you decide, your mind will never be one hundred percent convinced that you made the right decision. The nature of the mind is to be indecisive and doubting. Whatever you decide, your mind will question, "Did I decide right?" That's why we are inspired to go beyond the mind. If we could achieve absolute certainty of mind, we would never aspire to reach the state of mind-lessness or Divine Consciousness. We have to accept that as long as we are functioning through the mind, mind will have this dubious nature.

To handle a problem, decide to take action about it and then take the action, but know for sure that your mind will keep raising questions and doubts. Don't pay any attention. Once you have decided, tell your mind, "Shut up!" Otherwise you will keep changing your mind. When you go to your office, you may have a problem deciding what to wear. If you keep being indecisive, you will never get out of the house.

BE BOLD ENOUGH
TO MAKE
MISTAKES

EVEN DYING IS not a problem. What is the difference whether I die tomorrow or after one hundred years? If I die tomorrow, at least I have eight or ten hours. If I die after one hundred years, maybe I have eight million hours. The point is not when I will die but how I am going to live and enjoy those eight or eight million hours. If I lose myself in the celebration of eight hours, will I care how long I live? If I am not able to lose myself in even eight million hours, do I gain anything out of living? If not, even this span of one hundred years is a torture, and life is a problem: "I've got to raise my child, I've got to pay my bills, the car is always breaking down, I don't have the right clothes." Having a problem is only a matter of attitude, so handle a situation with a firm, decisive attitude. Swing back and forth, think pro and con—then decide and be bold enough to make mistakes.

The more you are bold enough to make mistakes, the more you move forward in the course of life. If you have to make ten decisions but make three mistakes, at least you have taken seven right steps. If you are unable to decide, you remain stuck. Be decisive, be bold, be courageous.

Have good intentions and be fearless; then, when you have made a decision, celebrate doing your best. If you make even the best decision and carry it out as if it were a big burden, there is no fun in life. We can always celebrate doing our best even in the worst situations. Two persons caught in the same life experience can go through it differently because of their attitudes, and we can always find something good in what others see as bad.

Two persons looked out through prison bars.

One saw the mud, the other saw the stars.

When I fight with someone, I tell myself I am seeing the mud; I'm not seeing the stars. Why put energy on the mud? Gradually we have to train ourselves to use this mud to make bricks of courage and compassion.

HANDLING
A
PROBLEM

WHEN YOU tackle a problem, you do things one of three ways: helplessly, compulsively, or willingly.

You go through a problem willingly if you are handling it consciously and decisively. You are celebrating. If you are going through a problem helplessly, you are acknowledging that no other course is possible. Even if you are going through torture, accept it and see what you can do about it. Remember that even in the worst situation you can celebrate doing your best. That attitude is your willingness.

When you are compulsive, catch yourself red-handed then and there. By catching yourself in the act of doing something you don't want to do or should not do, you resolve a certain amount of the problem. Because of your awareness, because of stepping back from the compulsiveness and watching it as something outside yourself, you are able to take the power out of the compulsiveness. When you identify with compulsiveness, you unknowingly energize it. When you watch your compulsiveness, you take energy from it.

If you maintain this awareness for a few days, you will

notice a difference in your behavior: You will no longer be compulsive. Awareness of the compulsiveness breaks the pattern. Through observation, you come to realize that most of the time you are not compulsive, and you are doing your best.

More far-reaching and important, you will realize that no matter how careful you are, you do become compulsive now and then. When you are caught in compulsiveness, your mind may play a trick on you, telling you that "I am not able to control myself, so let it be as it is." Don't develop that rationalizing attitude. The dignity of human life is self-control. If you have decided to and are willing to control yourself, you can. When you are not in control, you will have an itchy feeling, a sense of remorse. When you do control yourself, it is not for the sake of others; it is for your own growth and goodness.

Enhance your awareness and celebrate yourself. How wonderful you are for doing your best. Mind has convinced itself that there must be a problem. When you develop an attitude of acceptance and celebration, there is no problem. It is actually the attitude of looking at a life situation as a problem that is the problem.

Brooding drains you. Whatever you did, you did. It took perhaps five minutes. Why not celebrate the other twenty-three hours and fifty-five minutes? It is our awareness of celebration that determines the quality of our life. Life is like an ocean with waves and ripples, all having the same consciousness.

———————————

THREE
FANTASIES

THREE FANTASIES are possible: a life of luxury and comfort; a life of selfless service; or a life of peace, attunement, and freedom.

A LIFE
OF LUXURY
AND COMFORT

THIS IS A frequent fantasy, and within its limits it's perfectly acceptable. But it is ego-driven, and one of its limits is that it doesn't satisfy for long. It creates a desire for more luxury, more comfort. It's a fantasy that does not bring you closer to yourself.

A LIFE
OF
SELFLESS SERVICE

JESUS AND BUDDHA were the embodiment of service, going from place to place, from person to person to help, heal and comfort. Buddha taught, "You are okay the way you are. This problem you are having is only on the surface. Deep down, you are as wonderful as I or anyone else."

If we are really willing to serve, what do we need to own or achieve to be of service? Is it not simply our attitude that is important? If you have the attitude of serving, you can give a massage, share kind words, listen to others, offer a cup of tea. How many people just want to render such simple service? When you serve wholeheartedly, you are free of yourself. Although there are many humanitarians, their ego is dominant. That is why they complain they are "burned out." If you are simply an instrument of service, it doesn't matter whether you are a candle or a light bulb. The satisfaction is in the serving; your fullness and joy come from your selflessness. No matter how poor and untalented you may be, you always have this gift of being a source of comfort and joy to others. It depends only on your attitude and how you look at yourself.

A LIFE OF PEACE,
ATTUNEMENT,
AND FREEDOM

THERE ARE people in many religions who prefer to lead a contemplative life in peace, attunement, and freedom. They are like flowers wherever they are. If you come into the presence of such mystics, you receive their fragrance; but such mystics don't go here and there to share that fragrance.

If you attune to your focal point, you feel good about yourself, you transcend body and mind, problems and diversions. Meditation helps, but it is is a wrong attitude to be too concerned about the results of meditation. Real meditation begins when you start having fun with it. It doesn't matter if you are not able to concentrate. God is happy that you are doing your best, even if your mind is scattered. When your child calls out, "Mom ... Ram ... Om ... Tom ...," does the mother care whether the child calls her in the right way or the wrong way? It is the sound of the child calling that moves her; she knows that her child needs her. We all are Divine children. There is nothing to control. There is nothing to do. When we develop an attitude of total acceptance and celebration, there is no problem.

BEYOND DUALITY

WHEN YOU FALL asleep, your mind goes into inertia and leaves the world of duality. You can leave the same space consciously. As, in inertia, your mind goes beyond the duality of good or bad, right or wrong, so it can go beyond duality into pure consciousness. Whenever we feel joy, we transcend the duality of the subject-object relationship. Subject and object merge in oneness.

Is there any difference between eating and meditation? They convey the same joy. We say meditation is divine. We say food is an indulgence. These are only names we ascribe. It is the same.

In the beautiful words of a mystic, "When I am present, you are missing; when you are there I am missing. The lane of love is very narrow; two cannot stand on it at the same time." They have to become one.

You are fulfilled within yourself; your partner is fulfilled within himself or herself. Our attitude in relationships should be to go beyond the body and mind and provide the incentive and inspiration for one another through which to be in touch with our inner fullness and contentment. It is easy to turn our awareness toward beauty. It is not an effort to look at a beautiful face. It is spontaneous. To develop awareness is as simple as seeing. It is our attitude.

When we reach that state of consciousness, we feel the grace of the Lord manifesting through us as we are. It is manifesting through me as I am, through you as you are, through her as she is, through my finger as finger, through my eyes as eyes, through my ears as ears. Is it a problem for my ears to be ears and not eyes? Is it a problem for my eyes to be eyes and not fingers? It's all right to be just the way you are.

If you fill a cup, the cup will be full when it has a cupful. The cup cannot contain what a jar or pitcher can contain, but the fullness of the cup is the same as the fullness of the jar or pitcher. You may not eat like a tiger or an elephant, but when you are full, your fullness is the same as that of a tiger or an elephant. You may not be doing great things like Mother Teresa or St. Francis or Jesus or Mary. It doesn't matter. We don't have to accomplish things "like someone else." That is just our ego playing games. Measurement is a game of the mind. In the realm of spirit there is no measurement, only contentment.

Nonjudgmental Attitudes

THERE ARE certain concepts about charity, nonjudgmental attitudes, celibacy, and meditation that may be creating rifts in our psyche. We are all living on the surface, acting through masks. The concept of being nonjudgmental, for example, confuses us, since we are all seeking each other's approval.

Do you really care whether you have a nonjudgmental attitude? Get in touch with yourself and see. It has become a cliche to greet each other by asking, "How are you?"—but the person who first coined this phrase must have been a visionary, because this question reminds us to get in touch with ourselves. Unless we do, we might just respond, "Fine."

THE BEAUTY
OF
JUDGING

W E NEED THE ability to judge. Why do you bother to fix your makeup? How do you know when your face and hair are right? Do you care how you dress? When you go shopping for groceries, do you buy just any potato, any apple, any banana, or do you try to feel it to see if it is ripe, unripe or overripe? Would you like to be an animal, just eating and sleeping, unconcerned with any type of judgment?

The dignity of human life lies in being able to judge and evaluate persons and situations; but because you have heard that a nonjudgmental attitude is the Divine way to be, you seek a nonjudgmental attitude. Unless you learn *how* to judge and evaluate, you cannot go *beyond* judging and evaluating. You have to see the beauty of judging and integrate your life in light of your conclusions. Then you will automatically transcend your judging.

Let us make the question of judging more philosophical: Can you give up judging? Forget, for a moment, about how you judge others—can you give up judging yourself? You are constantly judging, "I am fat, my mind is restless, I am an alcoholic, I eat too much, I smoke too much, I should not fool around." You are unable to accept yourself the way you are. If you cannot accept yourself, how can you accept others and be nonjudgmental toward them?

You judge yourself as if you are different from what you are judging. You judge your actions, your thoughts, and your feelings—but how would you judge being? Should you be or should you not be? You read books and listen to lectures to find out how you should behave—but how should you be to be? It is easy for your mind to accept all this confusion as a way of security. You are secure in your meditation because it reinforces your confusion. What do you want to change within yourself, and can you change anything within yourself? Are you the doer?

How
Can You Fix
A Dream?

YOU ARE CAUGHT in a dream. In that dream, you are trying to fix the dream situation. How can you fix a dream? What would be the ideal situation in your dream? Can you ever be sure this is the ideal dream?

A dream is just a dream. The dreamer in the dream is not separate from the dream itself or from any situation in the dream. As the dreamer, whatever you try while in the dream is part of the dream. You cannot step out of the dream. By meditating, you realize how and why to give up on yourself. If you are sincere and serious about your meditation, you will realize that meditation leads you nowhere. Nothing leads you anywhere. As long as you think something can lead you somewhere, you are caught in slavery, imagination, and fantasy.

Through meditation, when you try your best and find yourself, you can give up on yourself; and when you give up on yourself, you transcend yourself. Giving up on yourself means you no longer use your intellect, mind, or ego. As long as you keep trying to fall asleep, you can't. When you give up, you fall asleep. The Divine Principle is like that. As long as your ego is active, whether it is active for selfless

45

service or for meditation, you can't get in touch with the Divine Principle.

———————————————

JUDGMENT
AND THE EVOLUTION
OF CONSCIOUSNESS

WHY DO YOU overeat? Do you overeat for the sake of making your cookies and cakes feel better? When you decide not to overeat, why do you not overeat? The purpose of overeating is the same as the purpose of not overeating—to enjoy life. The change is only in the dimension and depth of your enjoyment. Mother Teresa is enjoying sharing whatever she has. Those who are hoarding everything are also trying to enjoy. One person is at the stage of A-B-C by saving every penny. Another person is at the stage of X-Y-Z by sharing everything, but both have only one purpose: freedom and the enjoyment of life.

Many students do not care to study. They just fool around. Why? To enjoy life. Other students study seriously. Why? To enjoy life. The person who fools around does not see that the greater dimension of joy lies in studying. Even if that person could see that, he or she might not be capable of controlling compulsive habits of sleeping, drinking, talking, and so on. Each one of us is in a different state of evolution or consciousness, and each one of us is trying to find happiness by acting from that level. Everyone is equally sincere.

Can you judge a child, "Why are you a child and not an adult?" Can you judge a student, "Why don't you know A through Z the way I do?" It is normal for a student to be a student, for a beginner to be a beginner, for a child to be a child. In the same way, it is natural for your body to be as it is and your mind to be as it is. Our body is sometimes very grown up and looks old, but our mind is like a child. In the infant stage of consciousness, we don't know any better than to be jealous, fearful, deceitful, or cheating. We will outgrow that. Accept where you are, and from there see what you can do. If you get in touch with your Divine space of love, light, and joy, you can overlook everything.

In the beginning state of consciousness, we are just instinctive creatures. We accept because we don't know how to reject. Later, when our psyche becomes more developed, it becomes reflective and starts to evaluate: "What is real?" "What is unreal?" "What is true, what is false?" "What is lasting, what is temporary?" Then it starts judging itself.

A dog and a person may stand in front of the same mirror, but unlike the person, the dog will not respond to the reflection subjectively. The dog will not think, "I don't look pretty." The person's psyche has developed to a higher state. Without this judgmental attitude, you cannot really evolve. Thank God you have a judgmental attitude toward your looks and your eating and drinking habits. If it were not for thinking, there would be no electricity, no radio, no television, no communication. But if our thinking is clear, integrated, and evolved, we realize that the purpose of thinking is to go beyond thinking and to realize that dimension of consciousness which is all-peaceful, all-joyful, and free of thinking.

KNOWLEDGE
AND
WISDOM

THERE IS NO wisdom in information. Our wisdom does not depend on our thoughts. Thoughts, emotions, and desires all come and go like clouds. Wisdom is a space; it is forever intact. You are that space, that fullness which stays by itself and is beyond the clouds of thought, desire and emotion.

Don't build your wisdom on the basis of books and learning. All your Ph.D.s and degrees are useless there. There is no need to read books and listen to tapes. Just be yourself and enjoy your Self. If you feel like listening, listen. If you don't feel like listening, don't. In your real wisdom there are no words, no ideas, no fantasies. You are just yourself.

NEGATIVE SPACES
AND
COMPASSION

SUPPOSE I AM angry at someone or at myself. Can I switch over from the space of anger to the space of love and joy all of a sudden? So far, I have found it impossible. If I am really feeling hurt or angry, I cannot switch suddenly from the space of anger to the space of love, light, and joy.

Just as I get stuck in my negative space, others also get stuck in theirs. When you are stuck with your negativity, should I not have compassion for you? That poor fellow is stuck today like I was stuck yesterday and may get stuck tomorrow. What is there to judge, here? We all get stuck in different spaces. It is like not having enough gas in my car one day, and the next day seeing some fellow stuck on the road because he does not have enough gas in his car. So I give him a lift. When you are able to see your limitations objectively, you will have more compassion for the limitations of others. Even if you are very evolved, these limitations stay with you.

Appreciate yourself for what you *are*, because whatever you *have* is not yours. God is living through you and me, God is loving through you and me, God is aspiring through you and me to experience His/Her full glory. The reason you are hard on yourself is because of certain fantasies born of ignorance. You are already Divine. We all come from the same Divine Essence, and we are bound to merge in that Divine Essence. That was our origin. That is our destination.

May we experience the oneness of life.

May we experience a sense of relatedness with each other.

May we face every problem as a life situation good for our growth and learning.

May we celebrate doing our best.

May we remember that we can always do our best, no matter how bad the situation is.

———————————

PERFECTION
AND
IMPERFECTION

Y OU ARE VERY much aware of your imperfections, so I
would like you to be aware of your perfection too.

You think you are imperfect because you are greedy,
selfish, fearful, lustful, and lazy. But here comes a contradiction: Even if you don't believe you are perfect, you
believe something within you is so great and wonderful and
transcendental that you cannot compromise with anything
that is imperfect. You want to find that something which
is so profound, so uplifting, so overwhelming that it takes
you away from yourself so you can find that Self which you
really are. That is the real, universal Self to which each of
us is connected like rays to the sun. We may feel we are
lost; but no matter how lost we feel, we are always connected to that sun. That is why in the core of our being, we
all love Jesus and Buddha. We may not love Jesus for being
a savior but for what he exuded, what he stood for. We
adore any great person in any religion in any country
because that person somehow manifested the core of being
which is part of you and me.

To realize that perfection, we have to be in touch with
our imperfection. The greatest challenge for us as human

beings is being in touch with and accepting our imperfection. If we don't understand this concept of acceptance clearly, we may believe that acceptance will make us become complacent, self-centered, and unproductive; but it will not. If you don't accept, you cannot sleep. You may not be conscious, but this process of acceptance takes place in the flow of life. When you are ready to accept your selfishness, lustfulness, greed, or whatever weakness you have, then you are able to go beyond your ordinary state of consciousness.

THE CORE
OF PERFECTION
WITHIN

YOUR MIND SEES itself as a doer, an ego: "I have to do something, I have to accomplish something, I have to improve myself and contribute something to the world, otherwise I am living here in vain." Yet when you read great books about Jesus, Moses, or Krishna, they talk impersonally: "I am simply a channel, a vehicle. I am not really the doer; there is a higher force that manifests through me."

If this is true for those evolved souls, will it not be true for you and me? In spite of your imperfection there is in you a core of perfection. To get in touch with that, you need special training, a special path. The path may be different for different people. Perfection within you does not become more perfect because you follow a certain path. From a spiritual and philosophical point of view, even Jesus could have been a better singer, a better dancer. Even Buddha could have been a better wrestler, a better swimmer. Where is the end of this improvement? We will continue to improve, and there is nothing wrong with improvement; but something is wrong when we get too carried away with self-improvement.

CHOICES

WE ALL HAVE certain fantasies; that is our humanness. Whether we are very evolved or lost in mundane silliness, we are a little bit aware of fantasies. Just for fun, be in touch with your fantasies now. Fantasize the best form of life in which you could be your happiest with whomever you could be happiest.

What would you like to be doing when you are your happiest? Try to feel the nature of your fantasy, and you will find very interesting things. The root cause of your problems is confusion. When you are out of this confusion, you are in touch with cosmic love, light, and joy. See if you can feel this confusion. Don't resist it. Keep yourself a little open. Just get in touch with yourself and find out what would give you a state of fearlessness, guiltlessness, and freedom.

Today, in trying this visualization, I found three things. You might also find the same things, so we can compare. First, I thought of a wonderful house. As human beings, I think we all like to fantasize, "I wish I had a house in Hawaii or California by the ocean, etc." Next, I found I wanted a beautiful lover, very handsome and charming. Maybe you will not be satisfied with one; maybe you would like to have four or five. The third thing I found in my fantasy was freedom. I don't want any burdens. I don't want to be told what to do; I don't want to worry about my livelihood; I don't want to worry about having to give a lecture, maybe getting a donation, maybe not. Did you have that sense of freedom in your fantasies, that you don't want to be controlled and bothered?

Then, after these three fantasies, I asked myself, "Now that you have a beautiful home, a beautiful lover, and freedom, what would you like to do?" That was a hard question. I thought, "I would like to sleep as much as I want. I don't want to attend to any phone calls, just sleep." Then I thought, "I would like to make love as much as I want." Would you like to make love freely, to sleep freely? A third thought was more interesting: "I would like to meditate as much as I want and to write as much as I want because I love writing."

In your busy, burdensome life, do you get time to sleep? On weekends, most of us can sleep as much as we want. How many hours can you sleep, and how many hours can you make love in order to experience that ultimate satisfaction? Philosophically, if you realize that your body has to die someday, there is a limit to the number of hours, months, or years that you can sleep or make love.

The question of creativity and attunement is more subtle and complex. Most of us have certain passions, and these become creativity. When we find that space called freedom, we find that our creativity flows spontaneously. You are not happy with your life because somehow you don't feel you are able to manifest your creativity in a spontaneous, free way. Those who are spiritually inclined think in terms of meditation, prayer, and attunement. Those who are inclined toward creativity think in terms of writing, painting, or dancing. If you really want to spend time in attunement or creativity, what prevents you from doing that? If you could spend time in creativity and attunement, then there would be no fantasy that you would have to keep fantasizing. If you could reach your goal of attunement, creativity, and manifesting your potential, then why carry all these fantasies of someday having that house, that lover, or that freedom?

PHASES

YOU SPEND YOUR time in inertia, compulsiveness, attunement, or amusement. When you spend time in inertia, you are like a thing, a mechanical being repeating your daily habits without being aware of them. You drive without being aware of driving, you put on makeup without being aware of putting on makeup. What sort of life is that? If you are living in that fantasy house with that fantasy lover, you will have even more inertia. Thank God you don't have that fantasy house and lover. The more you face the challenges of life, the more your inertia is shaken and pulled apart. It is a great gift that we go through challenges and upheavals. We all have to do certain things we don't want to do. We need money for food, clothes, and rent, so we are helpless to avoid working for a living. We can do a little about breaking our inertia, but we are helpless about our helplessness.

COMPULSIVENESS

YOU MAY BLAME the social system for your poverty, but whom will you blame for your compulsiveness? Will you blame God? Will you blame your parents? Will you blame your teacher? As long as you are compulsive, you are not going to be happy with yourself or accept yourself. Don't think that you only eat or drink compulsively. These are gross things that anyone can notice. If you are spiritually inclined, you have to observe when you brood or fantasize or feel guilty or fear compulsively, and then you have to avoid these as much as you can. In the beautiful words of St. Paul, "What is that force which makes me do what I don't want to do and not do what I do want to do?" He was poetic and could express it in a beautiful way, but it is the same crazy compulsiveness. When you do something against your conviction and conscience, you are being compulsive. When you act according to your conviction and con- science—which means there is no doubt or conflict—you are doing it for your attunement.

You often do things as though you don't exist. When you feed your puppy or hold your child, be aware of doing it. Attunement means you are total; you are treating everything as if it were the expression of the ultimate Reality or Truth. You are attending to your "god." Here, god means your highest conviction, which you are pursuing in the form of doing your duty. Suppose that Jesus were to appear in person and that were to massage his head. If I am not total, I may think I should be giving a massage to his feet or his hands. If I am total, I know he is the same Jesus from head to toe, and he is enjoying the massage.

You often do things as if someone is forcing you: "I have to raise my child, I have to drive him to school, I have to bring him home." When do you really enjoy living? We should not live life as if someone is forcing us. Develop a sense of self-celebration. Whenever you do anything—including your meditation, your selfless work, your yoga, serving your husband or wife or children—do it with an attitude of, "I am doing what I should be doing, and I feel great because I am doing what could please the Lord the most." The core of attunement is to do what you want to do and like to do; to do your best; and at the same time to celebrate yourself for doing your best. Your best could be doing the dishes.

---

e

MAKING TIME
FOR
ATTUNEMENT

MOST OF US think we don't have enough time for attunement. We have time for jobs, girlfriends, boyfriends, picnics, traveling, reading and attending lectures— anything except attunement. We have to realize that nothing is more important than attunement, because no matter what you read or where you go or to whom you listen, ultimately you have to come back to yourself. Only by coming back to yourself and doing what you consider your best and celebrating yourself are you able to transcend yourself. Otherwise a rift remains: "I should have done it better; I should have done something different." Whenever you do something, be total. Be so total that the moment becomes the most important, most crucial moment of your life. Become receptive to that moment as if something very important is going to be revealed to you.

Attunement is the process of facing yourself and being yourself. You don't take time for attunement because there is nothing more boring, frustrating, and suffocating than trying to face yourself. Once you face yourself you find you feel lonely, bored, insecure, and confused; you find so many thoughts and fantasies, jealousies, fears, and guilts.

Who wants to go through that? So you turn on the television. You choose to spend time the way you do because that is the way you feel comfortable with yourself. Unless you realize this, you will keep fooling yourself; and if you keep fooling yourself, you won't be able to transcend yourself.

When you live according to your own truth and conviction, you feel either miserable or happy, but nobody is forcing you; it is your choice. If you enjoy it, you will automatically do a little more, because that is why you do anything in life—to be happy. If you enjoy being available to yourself for even one minute, automatically you will increase the duration. If you don't enjoy being available to yourself, you will know, "I feel so insecure, lonely, and disgusted that I have to get out of myself and read or watch television."

If this realization causes you to give up on your meditation or attunement, you will know that you avoid meditating not because you don't have time but because it is frustrating and boring. You also will realize that although it is frustrating and boring, it gives you awareness, wholeness, and self-mastery. Whenever you control your compulsiveness, you are bound to feel a little miserable at first. Whenever you do anything according to your conviction, even if you feel bitter at first, later you are bound to feel good about it.

DIVERSION

DIVERSION IS important for attunement. When you start meditating, doing selfless work, or praying, you find you cannot always keep doing that; you need some diversion. Any diversion you take with awareness is healthy and conducive to your growth, so don't think you are becoming compulsive or lazy if you take a diversion now and then. Go for walks, watch television, or play with your children; but know why you are taking that diversion. If you don't know, you are living in unawareness or being carried away by your impulsive, compulsive patterns.

You can have as much diversion as you want, but know that it is diversion—it is for fun, because right now you cannot work on your attunement, you cannot be loving and sweet to others. During the night, we all sleep. We don't earn any money while we sleep, yet we don't feel guilty for sleeping. Sleep is a must for the next day's creativity and attunement.

When I was a student, I was a sloppy, careless student for most of the year. Somehow I was gifted, so I could get high marks with only two weeks of study. While I was studying for those two weeks, my head would become exhausted after three or four hours of continuous study; I could not digest or understand anything and had to give up for a while. So I would go to a park, smell the flowers, play with the children, and watch all the beautiful faces. After ten or fifteen minutes I knew I could study again. If I had continued reading and studying at my desk, it would have been hopeless. When I took a little diversion, I opened myself for more receptivity and learning. Whether we are ordinary or extraordinary, healthy diversion is a must for each of us.

CONTRADICTIONS

WHEN I WAS living in a cave, I learned the contradictory nature of the mind. If people visited me in my cave, I felt annoyed that they were not leaving me alone to do my attunement and meditation. If they did not visit me, I felt annoyed that they were not giving me any moral support. I also realized that I was a bright student who was living in a cave and spending ten or fifteen hours a day meditating, chanting, and praying. Yet at night I was dreaming about women. This posed a problem. I wondered, "What am I doing? Why am I living in this cave? I should go and find some job, and a pretty woman; someone will find me appealing even if I am not very handsome. I should face some dangers, take some risks. What is this secure, sissy life? I should be more daring." Yet there was something within me that was more inclined for God, for enlightenment. I decided not to let myself be distracted but to save all my energy, time, and resources for this one purpose. So I continued.

DEVELOPING
ONE-POINTEDNESS

ACCORDING TO my understanding, in all of us there is a dark side and a light side. Only when you know your own lights and shadows do you develop compassion for other human beings because you know they are just like you.

When you understand the contradictory nature of your mind, not only do you accept yourself the way you are but you take certain measures to make your life more harmonious, more integrated, more refined, more balanced, more one-pointed. If your life is not one-pointed, you cannot feel happy, fearless, and powerful. You will always feel a little insecure, a little weak, a little distracted.

It is not that you don't have enough money or a beautiful lover; those are just excuses that you create because of your confusion. The real reason behind your insecurity is that your life is still not one-pointed. You have not been able to accept and harmonize your contradictory nature. You have been able neither to do what you could do nor realize that you could not do what you thought you could do. You have to know what you can do and then do it. Give up thinking about what you only imagine you can do. Once you have.

done this, you can't imagine how happy you will be. You will realize that it was just your own fear preventing you from realizing your creativity and attunement.

Let us not make fear mystical. Fear of what? Fear of losing what you already have or fear of not getting what you desire to have. You fear losing your car, boyfriend, girlfriend, or money; or you fear not getting recognition for what you are doing, a beautiful partner, or enough money. No matter what you have in life, you are bound to lose it, whether you fear or don't fear. Can I hold onto my youth forever?

What do you aspire to have? Do you want freedom? Freedom for what? So you can have a good time eating, drinking, smoking, and making love? If you could utilize even a little of your freedom, you could face the fires of hell. If you could be honest and use your freedom, according to your own conviction, for your creativity and attunement, then it wouldn't matter what else you had. You would become truly free.

Different religions are only signposts. In all religions the basic tenets are joy and compassion. Everyone wants to experience the joy of attunement and feel blissed out, to feel the joy of creativity, to paint, write, sing, dance, and enjoy self-victory. Sometimes you want to indulge in cigarettes or drinking, even though it is poison. If you do it as a victim of compulsiveness, you are bound to feel remorseful and guilty. On the other hand, if you indulge with a sense of self-mastery, self-control, and proportion, it can be a playful exposure, a healthy diversion that can enhance your attunement. So don't feel bad about your silly habits. Silly habits are very good for your diversion; but be watchful that those silly habits don't make you a victim of compulsiveness.

To deal with compulsiveness, know what makes a deep

impression in your consciousness, what pinches you. As a child, I fell in love with the candle flame. My mother tried to restrain me, but I put my finger there, and it burned. I remember that burning sensation and have never wanted to feel that sensation again. So, when you act compulsively, impose a healthy punishment on yourself from yourself. Be hard on yourself. Don't punish yourself just to build your ego: "I am fasting twenty days and have given up everything." Without making it known to anyone, punish yourself in a healthy way so your mind remembers.

Do you know why we behave? Because we know the consequences. Why don't we steal things from others' houses? Not because we are gentle and respectable, but because we know we will be put into prison and lose our reputation. Fear helps our growth. Thank God we are fearful! Do you want to be like those people who are walking the streets without any sense of guilt or fear? No, you like being a decent human being with a little bit of healthy guilt and fear.

As long as you are compulsive, you can never build self-esteem. Sometimes I punish myself by forcing myself to give away five or ten dollars to someone. Because I am so attached to money, it hurts when I have to lose five dollars for my silly compulsiveness. I don't mind if I have to give for a good cause out of large-heartedness, but when I lose money as a punishment for compulsiveness, it hurts.

Don't fool yourself that you are so great that nothing matters to you, so you can give this money away. That is nonsense. You are not that evolved. If you don't see your girlfriend or boyfriend, you feel miserable; if your car is towed away, you feel miserable; if the stock market goes down, you feel miserable. You are attached to everything of the world. Punish yourself wherever you are attached. Then carry out your decision as faithfully as you can.

CLARITY
AND
COMMITMENT

DO YOU THINK you will always be smiling like a Buddha? Who wants to be a statue like Buddha? My hand moves up and down; should it always remain still? There's no fun, no life in that. Life means movement, transaction, sharing, sensitivity. Movement means commotion, up and down. When you have that wisdom, you become free; you don't care about achieving.

Achieve only clarity. Clarity means freedom from confusion—knowing when you are being compulsive and when you are not being compulsive; knowing when you are enjoying your diversion and when you are enjoying attunement. If you are clear, you are doing your best.

Commitment means you go all the way, figuring out how much time you can devote, how much diversion you need; how, if you don't behave, you will punish yourself; how, if you do behave, you will give yourself some reward to inspire yourself more.

THE MELODY
OF THE UNFOLDING
PROCESS

KEEP IN TOUCH with yourself and define yourself in your own light. Maintain a journal. It is healthy to have an open dialogue with the mind. When I compare my notes of twenty-five years ago with those I make today, they are almost the same. I find the same crazy idiosyncrasies, and I laugh at my own notes. Yet there is some faint melody in the unfolding process also.

No matter how evolved we are, there is a little more we can evolve because evolving is infinite. When you merge in Cosmic Consciousness, there is no effort; but when you come back to your human consciousness, there is always room for self-improvement, growth, love, and joy. Be aware of yourself, celebrate yourself, congratulate yourself for doing your best. How wonderful you are.

This wonderfulness does not depend on any action. Mother Teresa is wonderful not because she is taking care of starving children but because of her attunement, dedication, and attitude toward her action. If you or I could have the same attitude toward any simple action, we would be as great as anyone ever could be. Greatness depends on our attitude, our awareness, our clarity, our freedom.

Right now, get in touch with yourself. Are you not happy and content? It is the same world as before. I have not given you money or gifts. If you feel different, it is because of your own clarity. If you feel content even for two minutes, can't you build a conviction that basically you are content by nature, perfect by nature? You don't really need anything to feel this perfection since it is your nature, your very being. You don't lack anything. You are perfect. It is different to want to go to the bathroom—but do you want the bathroom? You need neither girlfriends, boyfriends, money nor power because you are Divine. You are whole.

APPRECIATION

O NE DAY IN California, I was feeling lonely. Through coincidence or Divine grace, a cat who was usually very neglectful toward me jumped into my lap, and I felt so loved and accepted that all my loneliness went away. I realized how important a cat jumping on the lap could be even to a person like me, so proud of his wisdom, attunement, and meditation. A cat gave me a great revelation of how important love is to my life. When I was feeling depressed and lonely, its acceptance made me perky and cheerful.

What, then, about human love? What about others' gentle appreciation? If you are in someone's life, your contribution is very great. A student was sharing that she did not know how she could contribute to others. I said, "You have to contribute nothing. Just let others know that you accept them as they are. No one will feel more loved than by your giving them total acceptance." By accepting people as they are and giving them the freedom to be as they are, you offer them the best service. Someone is in your life; you are in someone's life. Know how important you are. Don't think how egotistical you are but how important you are to be touching and transforming someone's life with love and understanding.

LIFE
FORCE

D O YOU FORCE life to act? No, life forces you to act the way you act. You feel hungry in the flow of life; you dream in the flow of life. Do you grow your hair? Do you plan to think what you think, or do thoughts come and go? Do you choose to get stuck with a particular thought? When you fall in love, do you decide to fall in love? Just as you fall in love without planning with whom it will be, you get stuck with a particular thought that comes along. You only think you are choosing and deciding. When you are more in touch with your deeper nature, you know that you choose whatever you are ready to choose; you do whatever you are ready to do; you think whatever you are ready to think. You do nothing, yet everything is done by you. That is freedom.

If you could choose, would you choose to be lazy or to eat compulsively like a pig? Would you choose to lose your temper? You don't choose. It is how it happens. A child behaves as a child should behave. When you are more advanced in your spiritual growth, you come to realize you are simply an instrument, a vehicle. Life flows through you like electricity through a bulb giving light, a microphone giving sound, a refrigerator keeping food intact. The electricity is doing nothing, yet doing everything. In whatever form it is used, it does its job. You are doing whatever you are ready to do in the unfoldment of your consciousness. If you think that you choose, then choose what you think. Before you think, be sure it is what you want to think. If you find you are brooding or thinking compulsively, stop. You will gradually come to know that you have been acting as a Divine puppet. But this knowledge takes practice and awareness.

ELEMENTS
OF
RELATIONSHIP

IF YOU COULD choose just one relationship that was sooth-ing, comforting, inspiring, and uplifting for you—it could be your relationship with your dog, your cat, your child, your friend, your spouse, your parents—what would you say was special about it? Why were you so touched, so moved by that relationship? Would you like to have the same relationship with more persons? Would you like to stay in that space of peace and understanding?

We all are looking for a lasting relationship. We have to build our confidence and recognize that we have that capacity. Since we don't know how to relate to God or Universal Consciousness in the beginning, we start that process with each other. When we refine our sense of relationship, we ultimately transcend the relationship. We can avoid a relationship, but without going through it we are not going to transcend it.

To go to Chicago, you need a car or an aeroplane. First, you accept the car or aeroplane. When you reach your destination, you leave it. If you start out thinking, "Since I have to leave it, I am not going to accept it," then you are stuck wherever you are. First, you have to take it and accept it. Only with that understanding can a relationship unfold in a healthy spiritual way.

A relationship starts with trust. Even if you don't trust the other person, you have to trust yourself: "I will take a chance, I will go for it."

The second element is sharing. It is difficult to share what we have because we have put so much energy, time, and sacrifice into getting it. When a relationship requires sharing, we hold back; but if we intend to develop a relationship, we are required to share.

The third aspect of a relationship is learning to be. Being means being with someone without feeling self-conscious or dependent. The other person is like the fragrance of a flower or the light of the sun, and you just enjoy being in his or her presence. You are not required to perform; you are simply being. In these three phases of trusting, sharing, and being, love is present, love is underlined, love keeps refining the way that our relationship matures.

As long as you are only in two phases of the relationship, you don't get the cream. The cream of a relationship is realized when you reach a state where you can just be yourself. You have to be careful, because logically you might think, "If I am going to be just me and learn just being, why go into a relationship?" But that doesn't work.

In the beginning, we are like instinctive animals. A dog is being a dog; a cat is being a cat; a cow is being a cow; but where do they go? They are stuck in their instinctive animal life. Even this pen is being; everything is being. All are in the realm of being, but what do they learn? When you learn to trust, you go beyond your instinctive self-centeredness. You learn to share your time, energy, and money. But unless and until you have given the giver itself, your giving is centered around the ego.

This ego has its own mechanism to perpetuate the

illusion of separateness. It cannot feel great about itself unless it feels separate. "If I am one with all, then what is special about me? I want to be a great teacher, a great leader, a great humanitarian." The more we grow through selfless sharing, the more we see the shallowness of the ego.

When you feed your child, or your puppy or kitten, you feel joy. When you serve your spouse or someone else you love, something happens within your consciousness. You feel fulfilled, even though you have served someone who is separate physically from your body. As you experience that joyfulness, your ego melts. Then you don't *feel* joyful, as if you are the container; you actually *become* joy. Now the experience goes into a different dimension and is called a mystical experience. In that dimension you are not joy-full; you are joy, you are life, you are being. This is not only possible; it is the goal.

There was a monk in India who wanted to meditate in a wonderful cave. He went to a cave and meditated, only to find that his mind was still jumping and wandering. He decided, "This cave is not really the perfect one. Maybe a great saint did not stay in this cave, and that is why it is not working. I should go to a Himalayan cave." So he left that cave and went to another cave. After fifteen or twenty years, he still felt, "I don't know if the caves are holy or unholy, but as long as I have this crazy mind, I know for sure no cave is going to work for me."

Your relationship with your wonderful or hopeless spouse or friend is just like the relationship of that monk to the cave. You want to reach that ultimate state and have not been able to reach it, so you are blaming and changing your partners as he blamed and changed caves. How many times have you changed your relationships?

Before you start any relationship, it is good to have an

78

understanding of why you want to have one. Some relationships already are made for us. We are sons or daughters, brothers or sisters. The purpose of creating new relationships is to expand the horizon of our consciousness and enjoy the oneness of being. We have heard that there is something eternal, everlasting, infinite; but we don't know how to experience that or where to look for it. A relationship is a wonderful window through which you peek into infinity. Through selflessness, love, trust, dedication, and sharing, your heart becomes refined, and you experience that Essence which is beyond time, space or situation. It is great that you have someone in your life who can provide that window for you. In that space, you don't notice whether your partner is beautiful or ugly, rich or poor, smart or dumb.

Once, there were three beautiful lovers of Lord Krishna who had three different attitudes toward their relationship with Him. One, Vishakha, loved Lord Krishna because He made her happy. She was one of the great lovers. The other lover was Lalita. She loved Krishna because He used to make her happy, and she made Him happy. She was also one of the great lovers. The third was Radha. Radha loved Krishna because she could make Krishna happy.

This mythological story is an example of three attitudes we can have toward our relationships. We start where Vishakha was. "What can you do for me? What can you bring into my life?" We want to reach the stage of Radha but we are not there yet. It takes some time—and if we believe in the transmigration of soul, it may take several lifetimes—to reach the stage of Radha, but there is great hope for that. Our hope lies in the conviction that we are living and dying for love.

The beauty is in the journey itself, the journey of love. Brooks and rivers are flowing toward the ocean. You cannot say that they have no charm, no music. Even before they reach their destination, they have a certain energy, a zeal that inspires us and fills our hearts so that we love to go and sit near a river. Even if you are at the stage of Vishakha, even if you want your lover to make you happy, even if you love your lover because your lover makes you happy, convince yourself that at least you have that fire of love. We are here, we can reach there, but we have to trust the flow of life. Let every heart be running toward the ocean of love, peace, and understanding.

A relationship is going to work only when you are clear that, through it, you are going to grow and enhance your consciousness by developing trust and becoming more fearless. Otherwise you become too dependent on each other and end up not liking each other. You like someone because you like his or her company, but you grow to dislike that person if you become too glued, too dependent. Who wants to have that sort of mushy relationship in which you cannot breathe and you spend all your time wondering "Where is he, where is she?" You are drained by such thoughts. You have to make sure that you don't get attached.

For that purpose, learn to share your beloved—not in a gross, physical sense but in a sweet, Divine sense—by providing a space for the one you love to be herself or himself. It is good to be together to support one another, but it is good to be apart occasionally, to have some space free from each other. Then you know how you can handle yourself without that person. Sometimes he or she should go shopping with someone else so you can know whether you feel jealous and possessive. You come alone, you will go alone, and you can never be sure what will happen in life. To have a healthy relationship, have that space in which you are not constantly depending on someone.

It is not the purpose of a relationship to always make each other happy. We rub each other to polish each other, to shine each other. You should not just keep adoring one another and saying how wonderful you are. Sometimes you should lose your temper. It gives you a sense of freedom. Then, when you want to practice being yourself, let the person be there in your life as a fragrance or ray of sunlight and just ignore him or her. That is a more mystical way.

SENSITIVITY

ANOTHER ASPECT of a relationship is the ability to be sensitive to the other person's sensitive areas, whether that person is your brother, mother, sister, or friend. Someone might be happy if you are sensitive enough to offer a flower or a cookie, or to write a letter or call. Someone may feel very annoyed (although he or she may not tell you) if you turn on the light when he or she would have preferred the light off. Someone may be bothered by how you open or close the door or don't keep your room clean or leave the dishes. If you know this and take care of it, the other person feels loved and respected. Many times we become so preoccupied with ourselves that we don't think of what could make others happy. In a really good relationship, it is very important to know the other person's sensitivities.

———————————————

COMMUNICATION

COMMUNICATION is very important. You may take for granted that because you are with someone, he or she should know what you are really like, what you want to achieve, and what you want to share. What is wrong with telling each other? Be childlike. A child tells its mom, "Give me ice cream, give me candy, give me a balloon, I want that book." Let the child within you be childlike: "Could you do me a favor? I would like this."

People talk about jobs, about buying cars, houses, or new clothes; but they seldom talk about deeper things such as immortality, God, reincarnation, meditation, or freedom. Ask your friend, "What are you thinking, nowadays? Do you ever feel jealous, insecure, or tense? So do I. How do you cope? What do you do to be more playful?" Be open to sharing your thoughts, fantasies, and fears. The more you share your deeper feelings, the more you develop a sense of oneness. With proper communication and sensitivity, you enhance your trust and love for each other.

THE
RIGHT
ATTITUDE

YOU ALREADY have known many people and things in life, but unless the quality of your heart changes it doesn't matter what you have or with whom you keep company. This quality of the heart can change only by having the right attitude. Perhaps you already have someone you really love, such as your children. See God, Divine Essence, in them. See something in your child that you may not have in yourself, and let the child know you are learning about that from him or her. Then your child will feel really loved and respected.

If you have that quality of love, what are you missing? What can you lose? The only thing missing in life is love. We go through relationships to find that love which makes us transcend ourselves. Once we learn the art of relationships, we are always content.

No matter whom you meet, you are related in a mystical way, although the other person may not know it. With whomever you are related, be patient. Tell that person how grateful you are and what you have learned through him or her. Don't think the person will become arrogant. When you open your heart to the attitude of gratitude, to the attitude of learning, you uplift yourself and the other person as well. Each one of us has a Divine spark, a special quality. When you zoom into that quality, you are reinforcing the other person's confidence; you are reminding the other person of his or her Divine potential; you are inspiring the other person to take a chance to be himself or herself. That is how we learn to be confident and secure.

Once you start experiencing that melody of love, you look into my eyes, I look into your eyes, and we are related. We are here, we can reach there; but before we can reach there we have to trust the flow of life. Don't start the journey by blaming. Start the journey by appreciating.

———————————

FLATTERY

FOR A GOOD relationship, it is important to have mutual feedback. Sometimes we think it is just flattery, and we should not flatter; but even flattery—you can also call it complimenting—can be important and beautiful in a relationship. It is bad if you flatter with the ulterior motive to take unfair advantage of someone, but if you flatter with a pure heart, there is nothing better than simple flattery.

All your prayer and devotion to God is flattery: "How wonderful You are, how merciful and beautiful You are, smiling through flowers, flying through birds and roaring through the ocean." Isn't this flattery? We are encouraged to flatter each other so we can learn to comfort each other.

God doesn't care for our flattery. You offer everything to Him or Her who doesn't care, yet to one who cares you never offer. We are supposed to pray to God or flatter God so we can learn to flatter each other in a healthy way: "How beautiful your eyes are, I have never looked into your eyes before. Wow! " We need feedback.

Often the children are neglected if both husband and wife have to work. Children need special love and feedback. Treat your children as if they are God's sweetest expression in your life and have come into your life to bless you. Sometimes we treat them as if they are burdens, and because we cannot get rid of them we have to put up with them. Celebrate that they came into your life to open your heart. If you can treat them with tenderness and love them with openness and trust, you will have a Divine experience.

THE LETTERS
OF
LOVE

IN INDIA, children are not put to bed just because it is eight o'clock. When it is time for the child to go to bed, someone in the family goes to bed with the child. When the child falls asleep, the person leaves the bed. See the feedback given here. When that child grows up, how will he feel toward those parents who were so giving and supportive?

I am reminded of Kabir, who says, "There are many scholars in the world who are constantly studying scriptures, but none of them has become a really wise person. Only that person can become wise who learns two and one half letters, *"prem."* In Hindi, when we write "prem," which means "love," we use two and a half letters. Kabir is saying that a person only needs to learn the letters of love to become wise. In English, we have four letters, l-o-v-e. How much time do we give to that?

Many of you complain that you were not loved by your parents. There is no sense in complaining about parents. They might not have been given good feedback in their own childhood and were victims of whatever situations they were in. There is something wonderful in being a great parent. Wouldn't you like to be the type of parent about whom your children could feel proud? Then, when you are old and no longer needed, they would still feel that attraction in your presence, as though they were being charmed with Divine energy, love, and joy.

If we could change the setting and be wonderful parents, it would be uplifting for us as well as for our younger generation. How much time do we spend with our children? We spend time with television, with girlfriends and boyfriends; we spend time making money. We already have enough abundance, my friends. Now it is time for us to work on our love and selflessness.

Many people love to meditate, to go to seminars and retreats. You are running to a cave and meditating not because you really care for God but because you are still not able to see God in day-to-day life in your puppy, in your spouse, in your child. God is everywhere. God is in me, God is in you. Can you experience God only when you close your eyes?

When you appreciate tenderly, lovingly and joyfully, you not only help others whom you are appreciating and flattering but you help yourself in the process. By making someone happy, you become happy. You may become lost in the beauty of that experience. Ultimately, there is no other mystical experience than being lost.

LOST
AND
FOUND

WE GET LOST in two ways—either in compulsive pursuits, or in awareness of being. "Lost" means that this self-centered, body-conscious mind is no longer conscious of its limitations. It is as if there is a parrot in a cage. When you release the parrot for a while to fly in space, the parrot feels elated—"Wow!" Then the parrot comes back to the cage, but it has experienced the vastness of being.

When you please and care for someone, your parrot mind goes beyond its cage of physical boundaries and limitations. Never hesitate to find something sweet to tell your darling. If you are looking for a darling, start by finding something beautiful about her or him and zoom into that. Keep saying, "Wow, wow, wow, how wonderful you are!" The person may say you are the wonderful one. Finding beauty and complimenting each other turns into mutual love and creates a window through which you experience the Divine, mystical oneness.

Ramakrishna Paramahansa was one of the great mystics of modern times. He was a devotee of Mother Kali. There was a statue of Kali in a temple, which he used to worship. Through worshipping that statue of Kali, he became enlightened. He could feel the pulsation of Kali, not only in his own body, but also in the flowers and birds and walls and everything around him. First, he had to concentrate, to surrender; he had to be total in his awareness and devotion. He had to be absolutely faithful to that statue of Kali. When he mastered that art, the statue became alive and Divine for him, and that is possible in human relationships also. It is possible to realize the Divine through the purity of a relationship.

When you share with, have sensitivity toward, and experience mutual appreciation for someone, your life becomes joyful and you develop a sense of faithfulness. If you are scattered and distracted, how can the other person be always faithful toward you? The more you are sensitive, appreciative, faithful, and dedicated, the more your relationship shines.

ATTITUDE

WE ARE constantly judging each other: she is not pretty, he is not productive, she is not smart, he is not humorous, she is not creative, he is not generous, etc. We will continue to pick on each other to a certain extent, because that is our humanness; but we have to be aware of this picking habit and not allow ourselves to be victims of it. We forget that each one of us has limitations, and the other person's limitation is not his or her problem—it is your or my problem. Why? Because we expect something other than what that person can offer.

If you go to a plum tree and ask for bananas, how can the plum tree give you bananas? If you feel bad about it, then it is your problem, not the plum tree's. A few of us are like plum trees, while some are like banana plants or apple trees. Each one of us has something special and unique to offer. It is only because you are expecting something that the other person is not capable of offering that you feel hurt and annoyed. Let us not expect; let us accept with a grateful, appreciative heart what others are capable of offering.

In spite of your precautions and sincerity, you may find that things are not working. Certain relationships become so tied up that you don't feel the air of freshness and new growth. You have to be careful that you are constantly growing in your attunement, creativity, and freedom. If these are not increasing, something is wrong in your relationship. If you don't grow yet stay in that relationship, it may explode. Before it explodes, it is better to share your feelings objectively and frankly with your partner. Maybe the windows of communication have been closed too long and a fresh breeze is needed. When you share lovingly and peacefully before a situation becomes too serious, you may find that the other person is also open to changes.

However, sometimes there are limitations. When I was in California, there was a small dog who suddenly jumped into my lap while I was meditating. I felt annoyed and pushed him off. Then I felt bad because there I was, being attuned to Cosmic Consciousness, and the Cosmic Consciousness wanted to show me love and appreciation through the puppy. I thought I should not have behaved harshly, so I forgot about my meditation and tried to be friendly with the puppy. Half an hour later, I was doing my headstand, and the puppy came over and started licking my lips. That was too much. We have to admit our limitations. We have to be accommodating and open, but when it crosses beyond certain limits, we can say, "That's enough."

SELF-DISCIPLINE

IF YOU BECOME aware that you really are seeking freedom, creativity, and attunement, you will nurture a relationship in a healthy way. Before that, you have to have a healthy relationship with yourself. Even if you have the best partner, you may bring your own insecurity, selfishness, or jealousy into the relationship. You may not see that it is not the other person who is creating the problems, it is you. How can you know that your relationship with yourself is healthy? You develop a sense of self-discipline. If you eat too much, sleep too much, drink too much, or smoke too much, you will feel bad about yourself even if you are in heaven. You may have beautiful, curly hair, but if there are lice in it you will feel itchy. Bad habits will keep bothering you like a toothache.

You can get rid of these brooding thoughts and negative patterns only when you have a healthy lifestyle. For that, you have to eat properly, sleep properly, and if you have some drinking or smoking habits, control or moderate them. Do some exercise. You brush your teeth every day because you know that not doing it will have terrible consequences. Similarly, you need to take time for your exercises. Even if you have the best lover, the most wonderful parents, and the most angelic children, nothing will work unless you are happy with yourself. So far, I haven't found how to make self-discipline sweet, but when you accept that the discipline may not be enjoyable but you do it anyway, you feel victorious.

TIME

BE SURE TO have more than ample time for yourself. I don't mean that you should impose five or six hours of meditation on yourself, but have ample time for whatever makes you feel whole. If you can feel whole in a garden with the birds chirping, take time to sit in that garden. That is meditation for you; but don't fool yourself that you will continue to enjoy that. No matter what you enjoy or how much you enjoy it, you like to have a change.

You will not need more than an hour or two just for yourself. Then later, as you do what you have to do, you will not feel deprived. You will have a sense of wholeness: "Now I am open for it." We are seldom total with anything because we do not allow ourselves enough time to experience wholeness. Don't fool yourself that you are a great humanitarian, a wonderful wife, husband, teacher, or doctor, so you don't have time for being yourself because you are serving others. You help others more by keeping in touch with your own space of wholeness. We are running to fill the emptiness in our heart. If I could maintain that space, I would not have to speak, and you would be more benefitted with just my simple presence.

When you speak, see whether you are speaking out of compassion or out of emptiness because you want to get something from outside. There is nothing wrong in recognizing your emptiness. We all feel emptiness. That's why we share, communicate, and need relationships; but don't ignore the wholeness and fullness within yourself. Let your compassion flow from there.

When you take a shower, don't rush. This rushing element is very bad. If you can't take a shower for five minutes, take a shower for two minutes and realize that you have one hundred twenty seconds. In those one hundred twenty seconds visualize how many drops of Divine love and grace are falling on your head and shoulders. A mystical experience does not depend on the length of time or a particular place or situation. It depends on the intensity of your wonderment. The more you take things with that attitude of wonderment, the more you reach that space of bliss and transcendental unity. You don't have to have a relationship or meditate or be disciplined to recognize your wonderfulness. You can just be taking a shower, and the miracle may happen.

Eating

and

Meditating

TONIGHT AT DINNER, I closed my eyes as I was enjoying it. I remembered when I was a young boy, the older people used to tell me, "Food is a gift of the Lord—when you eat it, appreciate it wholeheartedly." At the time, I thought they were just trying to keep me quiet at mealtime by providing this nice philosophy, but the older I got the more I realized the beauty of it. Now, whenever I eat, I feel that eating is a sweet form of meditation.

If I don't enjoy what I eat, my belly feels full, but all day I feel as if something is missing. What is missing is that, through my eating experience, my mind did not reach that flavor of oneness and joy. My mind is not seeking food; it is seeking the flavor of oneness and joy. I don't love food, you don't love food, we all love joy and oneness. We try to fool one another with, "I love you." We don't love each other, we love joy. Let me experience that joy by either giving or receiving. Vishakha was receiving, Lalita was receiving and giving, and Radha was only giving. Each was experiencing joy. Through giving or receiving, we love each other to experience that joy.

Relationships are required only to open us for God's

grace. When you are open and whole, you show your love and admiration for your friends, relatives, and even strangers. Somewhere in that celebration, you transcend your individual consciousness and find that God is embracing you from all around.

PURPOSE
OF
RELATIONSHIPS

IN A RELATIONSHIP, you are required to act and behave in a certain way so that ultimately you can realize your pure being. What should you do to be yourself? You start with trusting, then move to sharing, and ultimately to being. Can you do anything to be yourself? Doing is required only for becoming, not for being.

When you discard fantasizing about becoming, you find being is here and now. It is because of your lack of self-acceptance, self-appreciation, and self-awareness that you are not seeing that you are Divine here and now. You are independent of your guilts, fears, and fantasies. They are all superimpositions on your Divine Essence. When you lose touch with yourself, you become overwhelmed by these superimpositions; but when you allow yourself to be yourself and saturate yourself with awareness, you transcend yourself in your universal Self, in which there is no guilt, no fear, and no fantasy. There is just the pulsation of peace and joy. It is all Divine.

When you open your heart, you uplift yourself, and you uplift whomever comes into your life. Once you experience that, you look into my eyes, I look into your eyes, and we are related. The more you share, the more you break the boundaries of ego.

Show your trust; learn to trust someone. Find out what you can trust, what you already are trusting. In some sweet, soft corner within each of us, we have a sensitivity for love and affection. The more you appreciate this, the more you feel inspired to reach higher dimensions by transcending all limitations. That is what you explore and aspire for through any relationship—with yourself, with others, and with God. Celebrate your wholeness, your oneness. Let all relationships merge into that.

BE GLAD
YOU FEEL
GUILT

I WISH YOU COULD dump your guilt and fear on me—but because you are serious and devoted, you will not do that. It is because of that shyness and hesitation that you are carrying all this garbage and not dumping everything on God. If you offer God only your goodies— your meditation and your prayers—where will you dump your guilt and fear? Either burn everything in the fire of wisdom or be humble enough to dispose this garbage somewhere. How long are you going to hide it?

This morning I went to the bathroom, then I went to the skyway, then to a great conservatory, then to a restaurant. When I went to the conservatory, I started to feel guilty. I saw the sweetest statue of Buddha and thought, "Oh, my God, if only I were like Him. Today I ate too much; I could not control even my tongue, and here is sweet Buddha with His eternal smile of peace and quiet." So I started to feel guilty.

Later, my host dropped me off at the skyway, and I took time to browse; but soon I realized I didn't have his phone number and didn't have any money. Suppose he had an accident. How would I explain to people who I was and where I needed to go? So I was fearful also. I went through the whole gamut. While I was feeling guilty and fearful, I was thinking, "Tonight I am to give a lecture on how to get rid of guilt and fear!"

Back at the house, they rang a bell to announce lunch. I took one or two minutes before coming, so that when I arrived at the table the others had to say their prayers again. I became very restless. I told them, "When I come to the table, I have to get food right away." They served the plates one by one. When I got my food, I forgot about everyone.

One of my friends was describing some of her weaknesses. I told her that I too am working on myself very persistently and faithfully. "My greatest failure is impatience," I told her. I am a very impatient person. "I have a great virtue also," I told her, "and that is that I have patience with my impatience."

When you are able to accept your impatience with patience, where is the problem? I went through guilt because I ate too much. I'll just digest it. I was fearful in the skyway, but now I'm relaxed. Where is the problem?

These are very normal feelings, not negative feelings. Without these feelings, you will not grow. They help you in your growth. Unless you feel guilty, will you care to improve? You will be happy the way you are. Thank God you feel guilty. The force that inspires you to grow is this pain of knowing, "I could have done better," and the determination, "I will do better." Thank yourself when you feel guilty. That is proof that you can grow and do better.

It is the same with fear. If you didn't fear a little, would you care about your education? With fear you learn to regulate your life. If you didn't fear, you would rob and do many silly things. Thank God we fear, otherwise we would be worse than beasts. Civilization is based on this fear. How many people would behave as they behave without being fearful? Thank your fear, thank your guilt, and enjoy yourself.

It is very difficult to enjoy yourself because you are expecting something great to happen in your life. How and when will that great event happen? You are intelligent and devoted, yet you think that at a certain place or time you will have this wonderful "ahhhhhhhh." Is my Divine Essence dependent on a particular place, time, and situation? What about this time right now? What about this place here? What about appreciating this situation?

If you said to me, "I am not feeling the Divine bliss, peace, and freedom I want to feel," then I would ask you, "Are you sure?" The more you are sure, the more you are clear. The more you are clear, the more you know whether you can or cannot do something, whether you can or cannot accept yourself, whether you are stuck or just playing the game of being stuck. Be sure.

IMAGES

THERE ARE TWO types of thinking: voluntary and involuntary. As long as you are not thinking voluntarily, don't feel guilty about involuntary thoughts. Those thoughts are just flying in space, just coming and going; you are simply relaxing, not looking for them. When you learn to differentiate between voluntary and involuntary thoughts, you reach that space of relaxation in which you detach yourself from thoughts and thinking. Once you detach yourself from thoughts and thinking, what is guilt or fear?

BREAKING YOUR IMAGE
WITH
YOUR OWN HANDS

IT IS VERY important to get rid of guilt and fear in order to share selflessly. Whenever you share selflessly, the very tonic of love will heal all your wounds of guilt or fear. You will experience being in a different dimension of oneness. When we create that melody of love, we forget our individual personalities.

Fear is attachment to security. You want to be sure your girlfriend or boyfriend, wife or husband is not going to dump you. You want to be sure you stay youthful and have enough financial resources when you become old. There is nothing wrong in planning and having money and a beautiful relationship, but going through these security measures is not going to grant you the security you are looking for. Even if your wife is very beautiful, can she maintain her beauty after sixty years?

We have no choice but to look in a different dimension of life—a dimension where love, beauty, and serenity are forever intact. For that, we have to get in touch with our deeper awareness which is beyond guilt and fear. If you let go of fears about the future and guilts about the past, what is left? Serenity. But you seldom appreciate that gentle, innocent space. Only in this space do you realize that guilt and fear are part of a dream. Now the dream is over, and you are in a free space.

Guilt and fear arise from a conviction you have accepted about yourself. None of us is really guilty, none of us is really fearful, but we have accepted that image about ourselves. Is your nose guilty? Are your ears or lips fearful? What is it within you that is fearful or guilty? It is simply an image you have made. You have to question: "Is this image real?"

What do you expect from yourself? You are fearful because you don't want anyone to find out that you did this or that. We all have done some silly things in life, and we are trying to cover them up as best we can. What will I lose if you know all my secrets? Simply an image that I wanted to project into your consciousness. When you learn to break your image with your own hands, you become fearless.

Not all holy men have been sweet, giving, kind, soft-spoken, and puritanical. Sometimes they were very temperamental. Durvasa used to lose his temper, Ramakrishna Paramahansa did not give up his tobacco, Swami Vivekananda smoked a cigar. Yet they were enlightened masters.

We don't have to defend our weaknesses by saying, "Well, if those great teachers had their weaknesses, I can certainly have mine." I am suggesting that in spite of your weaknesses you can realize your Divinity. There is nothing wrong in trying to get rid of weaknesses, but don't think that you have to be free of them before you can realize your Divinity. That is the point. You have laid a trip on yourself that unless and until you are free of this problem, you are not going to make it. That is nonsense.

Suppose the room is totally dark. You come from outside and stumble against some furniture. You might think, "I want light, but Divine light visits only holy rooms where everything is in order." You start fixing everything, and when you think everything is in order, you wait for light to dawn. Do you really think that anyone can fix the room properly without having light? As long as there is no light, you have to accept a little mess. You are thinking you should become so pure, so holy, so integrated, meditative, and generous that Divine light, God's grace, will shine on your life. You think you don't deserve that light because your life is not integrated; but that is why you *do* deserve it. Unless that light is there, you will not be able to integrate your life. The greatest trick of the mind is to keep postponing Divine light or grace with the excuse, "I am not ready." The moment you accept yourself with all your rottenness, that light is there for you. The trick is to get the mind to recognize and understand that right now you are all right. If mind will accept, mind will start losing its identity. It cannot survive without having some sort of confusion, some struggle, something to work on. If you have nothing to work on, either you sleep or you merge in Divine consciousness.

Suppose you reach that great height of having millions of dollars and all the beautiful girls or boys, so you are finally satisfied. Once you are satisfied, all guilt and fear are gone.

Now what will your mind do? Can you imagine your mind doing nothing?

Your mind will still create guilt and fear: "I am all right—but I am not yet like St. Francis; I am not like Jesus; I cannot heal; I cannot raise the dead." Mind will create something. If it doesn't create, it realizes its Divine core. You are simply preventing that Divine experience by creating guilt and fear, which is only a temporary condition.

The moment your mind accepts, it merges and loses its individuality in the universal Being.

BECOMING AWARE
OF
AWARENESS

WHEN YOU really get in touch with yourself, you accept yourself, but you do this unconsciously. You accept yourself whenever you are thirsty and get a cup of water. At that moment, you forget about guilt and fear, about not having a million dollars or a girlfriend or boyfriend. You even forget about God. You enjoy anything in life by accepting yourself, but you accept unconsciously.

I want you to accept yourself *consciously*. The greatest art of life is to do consciously what you do unconsciously at those moments. All spiritual disciplines are meant to awaken your awareness. You have to be aware because whatever you are aware of is simply a vehicle to bring your awareness to awareness itself. Only in awareness can your real beauty, real freedom, real Divinity, or greatest fantasy be found. When you maintain your awareness, there is something miraculous in the awareness itself. You don't have to do anything. If you put water in the oven, the water starts evaporating. If you are aware, all the fears, fantasies, and guilts evaporate. Nothing remains except awareness.

It doesn't matter what you experience. What matters is your awareness of the experience.

Most of us forget our awareness in the midst of experiencing the experiences. The normal way of enjoying life is to forget yourself into something you can enjoy: "Forget yourself, don't be self-conscious." But in a spiritual way you enjoy more by maintaining self-awareness. I am aware you are here. I am aware you are beautiful. I am aware you are attentive. I am aware I am peaceful. I am aware that I am.

When awareness and peacefulness merge, there is no distinction between them. In the beginning, you have to notice them, otherwise your forgetfulness of awareness is like anybody's forgetfulness in movies, boyfriends or girlfriends. But the more you get in touch with your own inner space where there is no complaining or pain of insecurity, the more you find that insecurity is simply a thought, a temporary feeling. Are guilt and fear really there? Where are they? If you move your mind, they are gone. You are stuck in your own images of guilt and fear, and these images are put into your psyche by society, by religions, by different conditionings.

Removing
Conditionings

THERE ARE certain customs, traditions, rules, and regulations wherever we are born. Our infant psyche has to grow somewhere in some conditions; but no conditioning is ideal, and every conditioning has to be removed later on. You have to stand on your own feet, so don't keep complaining, "My religion, my parents, my society did this to me." So what? Now you can be on your own, can't you? That is the purpose of life.

Even language is a conditioning. Through that conditioning we are able to communicate. Language is an understanding, a contract through which we can greet and interact with each other. Suppose you are a singer. I will enjoy your singing and not give a sermon at that moment; I will be quiet and listen. It is your turn to please me; then it is my turn to please you.

In India, we don't generally eat meat. If a swami were to eat meat, people might think, "Oh, my God, he is a religious man and eating meat." Yet many people are eating meat without feeling guilty. It is conditioning.

If you kill someone, you go to prison, but if you kill one hundred people fighting for your country, you will get a reward. People will say you were a hero to kill so many people. This too is conditioning.

Learn to be aware of yourself and thank guilt and fear when they come into your life. If they never come into your life, you will not question where you stand and will remain dead while you are alive—"dead" in the sense that even when you have your pleasures and comforts, you will not be aware of being alive.

Whenever pain comes, you have to go through it. When you don't have pain, either you are pursuing some silly pleasures and involvements and are not aware of yourself, or you are sleeping. When pain comes, you are jolted. When it is too painful, you will be lost in the pain and lose track of your awareness; but when the pain gets milder, be clear that it is milder. That is awareness. When you are not feeling negative, celebrate your positive feeling, your loving heart. Any pain or problem makes you more alert, more awake. You know where you stand and can question, "Can I feel better? Can I experience something higher? Is there a higher purpose in life?" The more you face this question, the more you integrate yourself and the more you maintain awareness of yourself.

Your mind can find temporary rest in senseless excitement, or it can be given a focal point. During meditation your consciousness is at rest. Enjoy life in your restfulness. In the beginning, a focal point is a must. When your mind is in that focal point, celebrate madly! The one who is celebrating will get lost in the celebration, and that will turn the whole perspective of life upside down. You will have a Divine experience or enlightenment.

As long as you are there to celebrate, keep celebrating. In the process of celebrating you will lose yourself in Divine consciousness, where there is no trace of guilt or fear, no trace of individuality. Don't hold on to your individuality if you want to shake hands with Divine consciousness. The separate self is looking for security without being willing to lose itself. Let go. Let your body remain intact and alert, but let your mind hang loose. In the process of letting your mind hang loose, all questions and doubts will be resolved. Do you want to be that type of mother who holds her baby so tightly that the baby suffocates? Like a good mother, keep watch over your baby mind, but let it be free. You have been repeating mantras, reading books, and going to lectures so that you could avoid facing yourself. If I tell you to turn your head and see the sun, the moment you see it you may forget to thank me because of the beauty you are seeing in the sun itself. If you see, you see. It doesn't matter who saw it first.

A LITTLE AWARENESS
IS ENOUGH

THERE IS A misconception that you have to "increase" your awareness. Where should awareness reach? You create this problem for your psyche by imagining certain standards. Suppose I am having some tea and cake, and you ask me, "Swami, are you enjoying it?"

"Yes," I answer, then ask you: "Can I enjoy it only this much, or should I enjoy it more?"

"Are you full or not?"

"I am feeling full, I could not eat it all."

Why are you concerned about eating everything in the whole cosmos? Maybe you will die if you eat everything. The question is whether you are full or not. You don't have to drink ten bottles to get drunk. If you are drunk with one cup, that is enough. The question is not how many cups you drink, the question is whether you are drunk or not.

You don't have to have so much awareness. A little is enough. You are practicing awareness of awareness as much as you can. Enjoy that. You don't have to be more aware than you are. When you accept your awareness as it is, there comes a mystical turn in your consciousness, and you transcend awareness.

Self-Mastery
Is
The Greatest Gift

YOU HAVE TO be in touch with yourself in such a way that you find out whether having a little diversion ultimately is good for your meditation or is taking away your energy. You have convinced yourself that when you are watching a movie, you are going away from God. Maybe when you are watching the movie, you are getting ready for more God. Maybe you are watching television too much and wasting your energy—or maybe you are taking a little diversion so you can be more seriously meditative, more giving and charitable. You have to keep an open mind and see whether this fun is really worth pursuing or will bring you gloom and agony later on.

When you drink consciously and intentionally, there is no guilt about that; but when you drink compulsively and too much, you are no longer master of yourself but a victim of your own desires and emotions. That's why you feel guilty. The most lasting gift of life is to have mastered yourself. Once you are integrated in your own light, you automatically enjoy serenity of being. God does not have to come from somewhere to make you happy. Your integrity will shine and exude that Divine fragrance. Fragrance *comes* from the flower; the flower does not borrow the fragrance. Divinity, the freedom that you are looking for, will come automatically from within you. You will wonder, "Why was I so tense?" If you were lost in the forest in your dream, do you question why you were lost there once you are awake from the dream? Once you are awake, you dismiss it. When you can dismiss guilt as you dismiss dreams, you are free.

———————————

DISMISSING
THE
DREAM

WHEN YOU ARE lost in a forest in your dream, how far are you from your bed? When you awaken from your dream, do you consult any maps to figure out in advance how you will never again get lost in your dreams? You don't care about maps because you know that even if you get lost in a dream, you really don't get lost; even if you get killed in a dream, you really are not killed. You know in the core of your being you are not affected by any dream. Similarly, if you occasionally get stuck in a negative emotion or thought, you learn to dismiss it just as you have learned to dismiss your dream.

SECURE
IN
INSECURITY

THERE IS something called Golden Silence. In that Golden Silence, your heart blossoms in Divine bliss. If we start talking and arguing about silence, we cannot experience it. To create this Golden Silence we have to keep quiet. Silence is there. Most of us prefer to be great doers, performers, and actors, but what should we do to create quietude? If we believe in doing, we merely stop talking. We can do not-talking. As silence belongs to shutting our mouth, Serenity belongs to shutting our brooding. When you stop brooding about guilt, fear, past and future, then you have Serenity.

How can you stop brooding about the future when your future feels insecure? Well, whose future ever was secure? Jesus was crucified. Socrates was given poison. Gandhi was shot. Mother Teresa does not have millions of dollars in her bank account. What is their security? Men and women of wisdom are secure in their insecurity. As long as you are not secure in your insecurity, know for sure that you are an ordinary person. Only when you are secure in your insecurity are you a liberated person.

Who can give you guarantees about your health, looks, or partner? Can you give yourself a guarantee about even your own mind? You feel one way in the morning, another way at noon, and another way in the evening. Can you love yourself constantly? If you cannot love yourself constantly, can you expect your wife or husband or children to love you constantly? Mind is fooling around. Body is decaying. The moment you can be secure in spite of this, enlightenment is for you.

You imagine that one day you will be fixed in Divine consciousness. But to have the human sensitivity of love, compassion, beauty, appreciation for flowers, birds and fellow beings your mind has to be as it is—going a little this way and a little that way. When you dare to be secure in spite of these insecurities, then you are ready for enlightenment.

———————————

SERENITY
IS
IN THE BATHROOM

LIBERATION IS freedom from confusion. Suppose you love someone. You have found a beautiful girl or boy, and you have fallen in love. You arrive at that person's home and knock on the door. The door is opened by some other person who tells you that your friend is in the bathroom. What will you do? Will you flirt with the third person? Or will you just wait? Maybe your beloved Serenity is in the bathroom and you have to wait a little. But you are too impatient. If you really love him or her, you will wait. If you are flirting, you are not ready for your beloved Serenity.

If anyone has found Serenity, you also will find it. Serenity is universal, but you think that because you are not holy you won't find it. Whether you are holy or unholy, virtuous or sinful—even if you are an animal—the sun shines everywhere. If the sun does not discriminate about sharing its light, will the Divine light discriminate? It is only you discriminating against yourself when you think you don't deserve it. You go to bed every night and expect to fall asleep. Do you think you don't deserve sleep because you have flirted with someone? It is your sense of unworthiness that deprives you of the experience of Serenity. Just have patience. Serenity is in the bathroom.

———————————

DOING
IS FOOLING
YOURSELF

YOU ARE ALWAYS thinking in terms of doing great deeds.
But doing is the best form of fooling yourself. What will
you do to be yourself? Should you meditate more? Should
you do the headstand, go to more lectures or read holy
books?

Be yourself. Don't let teachers or books confuse you.
Build confidence in yourself. If God or Serenity or Divine
Essence is a reality, it is within you. Let it manifest through
you.

You can do things only to obtain things from outside.
You can do things to get a job, to get a car, to buy clothes.
You should know you are doing things not for Serenity but
for material comforts and urges. You will get whatever you
get according to merits, intelligence, capacity, money, etc.
But can this Serenity be bought? Can Serenity be pursuaded
or charmed by your looks or gifts? Can you make a bargain
with Serenity? It is like that Golden Silence, which manifests when we are just silent and don't talk. Serenity is
always here and now.

You may think, "Then I can keep drinking, smoking and
fooling around." But is that being yourself? Being yourself

means awareness of yourself as you are, without doing or thinking. Actions, thoughts, and feelings are ornaments, attributes that are imposed on you or chosen by you. Find out whether you can be aware of yourself without thoughts and actions. Feelings, thoughts, and emotions are fleeting. Awareness is your very nature. When you are in touch with your awareness, you are in touch with your Serenity. Awareness, Serenity, and Divinity are only different names for one thing—your pure, universal Being. Get in touch with yourself, and when your Serenity is in the bathroom, wait. (Unless you would rather flirt with the other girls and boys called guilt, fear, and fantasy.)

EXPERIENCING
ONENESS

WE READ BOOKS to learn how to be holy, virtuous and pure. The books have validity, just as clothes have validity, but the health of the body does not depend on the clothes. Realizing your Serenity does not depend on puritanical or nonpuritanical attitudes. Serenity is a reality of every moment for every one of us. When you get in touch with Serenity, you automatically manifest a virtuous life because you can see better and you are more fearless. You are more loving and kind because you have realized a dimension of consciousness in which there is no trace of individuality. Everything and everyone is merged into oneness. Who is separate from you?

When I started my lectures, I did not expect I would fall in love with you. I was just flirting. I didn't know I would be trapped in my flirtation. That's how it starts in life, so be watchful! When you get a puppy, for a few days it is a lot of trouble to train it; but after a week or two you fall so deeply in love with the puppy that if it doesn't feel well, you also don't feel well. You would do anything for your puppy (or your kitten), as if it had become an extension of yourself.

We experience oneness by extending ourselves beyond the normal boundaries of our sensual nature. That is how we feel love and how even a puppy or a kitten can become an extension of ourselves. That is one of the greatest miracles of life. When you start anything with good intentions, you may not feel deep love in the beginning, but automatically you will feel it later; and when you feel it, you experience life in a higher dimension.

When you make someone happy, you really make yourself happy first. If I want to put perfume on your cheek with my finger, I have to first enjoy it on me. Can I rub perfume on your body if it is not first on mine? Just to visualize that I am going to make someone happy makes my heart happy. Go out of your way to make someone free from guilt and fear, and you will enjoy your life in a higher dimension. No matter how great we become in our life, it is a healing experience for the ego—which is the instrument of expression and sharing—to love and to be of service to someone. Always feel free to share your experiences with your friends and to let them know they have been helpful to you. We never get tired of being the focus of attention and love. It is great to meditate, but put into your life certain selfless actions and sweet, complimentary words, and you will find that your life is filled with beauty, love, and Serenity.

Your Life
Reflects
Your Convictions

IF YOU CANNOT prove with your life that you can shine, that you can be selflessly loving, how can you inspire the children who are looking to you to set a good example for them?

There was a mother who asked me, "Would you be kind enough to talk to my children? They never go to the temple or any holy place, and I am trying to persuade them so they will open their hearts to these good teachings."

I agreed to see them. When they came, I asked, "What are you studying, what is your goal, what do you think of God and spiritual pursuits, and why don't you feel inclined to go to the temple?"

They said, "Our mom has been going there for ten years, and we don't see any change in her personality. She has the same temperamental attitude. We think if we also go to that temple, we will be stuck like she is. We don't want to get stuck, we want to grow. If we had seen any change in her, we would have been inspired. Now, you tell us what to do. Should we go to that place where we know our mother is stuck, or should we find some other place where we know we can grow?"

I told their mother what they had said and asked her, "What do you have to say about this? At first, only your honor was at stake, but now my honor is also at stake. I talked to them, and this is how they replied. This is a challenging dilemma!"

The woman said, "That's true. What do you suggest?"

I told her there was only one chance: "You have to prove with your life that you can change. They are complaining about your temper. If you can prove that you can control your anger, I will be able to show my face to your children. Otherwise, no more invitations to your house. I don't deserve to come anymore."

I shared with her how I had gone through this hell of anger and told her certain tricks. She tried sincerely, and within one month she brought about such a change in her life that all the family members were shocked. Automatically, they all started going to that temple. Later, when I visited them, they said, "It's a miracle. What did you do? How did you change our mom?"

The point is, we are meditating and going to churches and reading holy books, but if we don't exemplify a certain serenity, freedom, selflessness, fearlessness, peace, and quiet in our own lives, how will others who are more in the beginning stages feel inspired to learn these things? For your own good and for the good of your children (even adults who are still children inside), you have to prove your convictions with your life. If you only "understand," no personal sacrifice is involved.

THE RIGHT
TO BE
DIVINE

SO DEVELOP A sense of self-discipline for your own good health, your own well-being. And go out of your way to help fellow beings. Don't worry if you are considered foolish. The day you realize your foolishness, you become wise.

The mind will always be foolish. It takes tremendous courage to realize one's foolishness. When you recognize the foolishness of your mind, then wisdom automatically dawns because you see that you are not the mind. Mind goes through all these ups and downs. Sometimes it is loving, sometimes resentful, sometimes fearful, sometimes lustful, sometimes meditative, sometimes giving, sometimes cheap. Can you build your identity on the basis of this fluctuating mind? When you no longer base your identity on your fluctuating mind, you are a free person. Once you see that, you become spontaneous; you don't carry an image of how you should act so that others think you are very wise and holy.

If you are married, do you go to church every day to get married? Are you constantly marrying and kissing to be sure you are married? Are you constantly looking at your reflection in the mirror every moment to be sure you didn't lose your face?

The way you know these simple things is the way you know you are Divine. When you are established in your Serenity, your Divinity, you are able to accept the changing thoughts, desires, passions, and idiosyncrasies that surface in the space of your consciousness. When you accept, you become lighthearted.

If you are caught in your expectations, you can't take work as play. Unless you can take your work as play, you are still too much identified with your image and feelings. Great masters are doing great things for mankind and working harder than you and I, but they can take those actions and works in a lighthearted way, in a playful spirit. In our Indian philosophy, we are told God created this world out of *Lila*, playfulness. Yet the moment you become playful, you start feeling guilty. If you really love and trust God, can't you be playful in showing your loyalty to Him or to Her?

The more you get in touch with your feelings with total clarity, the more you find you are released from all bonds of guilt, fear, and stupidity. You are pure Divine Essence. Great masters have been telling us that we can get in touch with the Master within us, we can get in touch with our Divinity. Yet you are constantly saying, "No, no, no, it is not for me, I don't deserve it." See clearly that to be Divine is your first and foremost right, and you are divine right now. If you are not feeling divine, see what you are feeling, and see how long this feeling stays with you.

Finally, maintain good company and associations. It is very important to have the right feedback. When you meet with gambling, you think about gambling. When you pass a grocery store, you think about food. You are lucky to have a spiritual center in your city. When you pass through a holy center, automatically you think about your awareness and the real goal of life. It reminds you of your own inner beauty, inner joy. Try to keep in touch with that community. You have to keep in touch with someone, so keep in touch with those people who are loving, selfless, and fearless. Automatically something clicks within you and challenges you to be like that.

Read the lives of great women, mystics, and masters because you too have that seed of Divinity. When you read about great lives, something within you gets churned up, and you question, "Can I feel like that? Can I be great like that?" Something challenges you, and all of a sudden you get in touch with your greater potential.

GUIDED
MEDITATION

NOW, LET US meditate together. For two minutes just get in touch with yourself and enjoy yourself.

Let your focal point provide a comfortable bed for your mind … Let your mind be restful and relaxed in the Divine, cozy bed of your focal point … Thank yourself and thank your mind for enjoying its chosen focal point …

See how sincere you are, how integrated you are … You are doing your best right now … You are totally integrated … Even if your mind is not totally attuned, at least you are putting your energy with total sincerity and dedication: "I don't care for enlightenment as long as I have this joy of attunement … As long as I have this feeling that I am putting my energy in the right direction, I am content and happy." … You are so happy with this feeling of total dedication that you forget about enlightenment and realization … Maybe this realization is enough for you … You are doing your best … Let your mind stay with its focal point … Let your heart smile in joy … Let your heart dance in gratitude … Let your being be saturated with ecstasy …

You want the whole world to love and adore you, but you never take time to love and adore yourself … How can the world adore you if you don't adore yourself? ... The world only follows your example ... Give an example to the world that you can adore the Divinity within you by being faithful to your own focal point ... your own wisdom ... your own understanding ...

Right now, you are not compulsive ... You are celebrating the dignity of human life ... You may not hear my words, but keep on celebrating yourself ... When you feel bored, accept this boredom too ... Without contrast, we cannot enjoy anything in life ... It is only through boredom that we enjoy dynamism and bliss ... Without pain, you cannot know what joy is ... Without resentment you cannot recognize what peace and love are ...

Whatever surfaces in your consciousness, accept it and bless it ... Don't resist it ... Don't fight it ... Give all liberty to God within you to manifest as He or She or It pleases ... Are you the creation of yourself? ... You are the creation of that Divine Essence ... Your thoughts and feelings are the creation of the Divine Scheme ... When you judge your thoughts and feelings, you are judging the Lord within yourself ...

You may put one hand on your belly and be aware of your breathing ... When you breathe in, see how your belly expands ... When you breathe out, feel with your hand how it contracts ... Keep in touch with your breathing, and through the awareness of your breathing you will be able to maintain awareness of awareness itself ...

Now release your hand and relax in yourself ... See how you feel—tender ... relaxed ... sweet and peaceful ...

If your mind wants to maintain the awareness of the focal point, let it maintain awareness of it ... If your mind does not want to maintain awareness of the focal point, let your focal point go ... Let your mind hang absolutely loose ... Trust yourself ... Celebrate the freedom of being ... You deserve it ... Don't hesitate to accept it ...

Now, for one minute let us chant Om ... Om stands for Cosmic Love, Cosmic Awareness ... Try to visualize that the sound is coming by itself ... You are simply floating on the ocean of the sound of Om ... You are not making an effort to make the sound ... It is coming on its own ...

Let us try ... Let us flow freely on the ocean of sound, Om ... Keep it unbroken ... OoommmOoommm-OoommmOoommmOoommmOoommmmm ...

Now, silence!

Rub your palms. Put your palms around your face. Gently open your eyes and observe the difference in the quality of your feelings and perceptions. You are the same person, having the same amount of guilt and fear—but does it matter? How relaxed you are about yourself. Look around freely without thinking anyone is there. It cannot be put into words. You have to experience it by yourself. Your Divinity is like a flowing river. How can you catch the river? The river is just flowing.

FREEDOM
AND
SELFLESSNESS

WHETHER WE believe in God or not, whether we believe in certain ethical values or not, we believe in the concept of freedom. If we are not free, it means that something is binding us.

What is binding you?

For many of us, freedom means not having outside pressure, not being obliged to do anything. Most of the time we imagine that freedom means being able to retire. But we cannot know clearly what spiritual freedom is unless we are exposed to a very deep, overwhelming experience of contentment. You may have that experience today, or you may not have it for several years, or lifetimes. No matter how ignorant we are, this longing for freedom is in our hearts. Freedom does not request us to strive for it. The search for freedom is inherent and irresistible.

FINANCIAL FREEDOM

THIS QUEST FOR freedom is experienced at different
levels. The first and foremost freedom is financial freedom—survival. Although I come from India, a poor country,
I have not found people's attitudes and behavior here to be
financially freer than in my native land. Americans have
better facilities and greater wealth, but I don't sense a
psychological freedom regarding financial security.

Do you have enough money for a year? If not for a year,
do you have at least enough for a month? If not for a month,
at least for a week? If not for a week, at least for a day? If
not for a day, at least for an hour? If not for an hour, at least
for a minute? If not for a minute, at least for a second? If
you can answer yes to any of these periods of time, get in
touch with that freedom for a second. There is something
very mystical about it. Freedom is like blasting an atom.
That tiny second has so much energy within it that when
you penetrate it with your awareness, you go beyond time.
It is the penetration of that moment that takes you beyond
time, and it is in that timeless zone that you realize what
freedom is.

I am absolutely in favor of abundance, prosperity, and

creativity. I appreciate people who are dynamic and productive; but I wonder what is missing that they don't feel secure. I have met many people who were very poor, just hand-to-mouth, but they gave me the impression of being content, cheerful, and happy, while rich people often seemed fearful and insecure. Even when I met millionaires, I sensed some sort of fear. So a lot of abundance on the material plane does not necessarily give freedom from insecurity and fear.

Fear arises in two forms. Either you fear losing what you have, or you fear not getting what you want. But how much do you really need? Suppose that you have a small piece of paper. If you are a good artist, you can make a good drawing on that small piece of paper. If you don't know how to draw and have even a huge sheet of paper, you will make a mess. Be aware of those people who do not have lots of material abundance but who have richness of heart. Material abundance will never provide you with freedom.

EMOTIONAL
FREEDOM

THE SECOND freedom is emotional freedom. Have you ever loved anyone? Have you ever hugged anyone? Have you ever rocked a child to sleep? Whenever you are in touch with that sweet person, go beyond your insecurity and celebrate yourself. Enjoy simple things with as much awareness as you can. Develop the awareness to see God in everything and everyone. God in lasagna. God in pizza. If God is really God, God must be everywhere.

Emotionally, we are insecure. We look for someone who will inspire us and give us loving support and recognition. However, others can give us support only to a certain extent. Furthermore, we can never be sure that others will be loving, supportive, and inspiring all the time. This is good—if you found someone that dependable, you would become attached to that person and never be inspired to seek within yourself the real Source of security. Whenever you become dependent on any person, you lose the sense of security that you should have within yourself. You are not looking for dependence—you are looking for freedom. There is nothing wrong with giving and receiving support, but there is something wrong with expecting too much from others.

Even my own mind does not always support me. Sometimes it is critical and judgmental. If my own mind is not always dependable, positive, and inspiring toward me, how can I expect someone else to be? In our quest for freedom, we should not give anyone unnecessary power to reveal freedom for us. We have to find it by ourselves, within ourselves.

SPIRITUAL
FREEDOM

IF WE CANNOT be free and happy with material abundance and emotional support, what else can we do? We can turn our attention toward spiritual attunement, the third freedom. Most of us like to see ourselves as really spiritual, but in reality we are only looking for comfort, money, power, and emotional support. Only when you have enough comfort, money, power, and emotional support can you aspire to spiritual freedom.

How can you know whether you are really spiritually inclined to divine freedom, or just flirting with material and emotional freedom?

I once knew a very intelligent man who used to discuss philosophy and mysticism with me for many hours. I was impressed with his seriousness. One day I said to him, "You seem to have so much compassion for mankind and zeal for God-realization. What time do you get up? What do you do all day?"

He answered, "I go to bed around ten or eleven and get up around eight or nine to go to work."

I asked him, "If you have this great concern for humanity, could you get up an hour earlier and help others or pray during that time to feel oneness with God?"

And he said he would try it.

One week later, we met again. He reported, "I tried, but I could only get up fifteen minutes earlier."

By the following week, he was rising half an hour earlier. But he admitted that he realized his zeal for mankind and God was simply a delusion. "If I am not keen enough to sacrifice even one hour of unnecessary sleep for God-realization," he said, "I have been fooling myself that I am so concerned about humanity and God."

When I lived in a cave, sometimes I would be very disciplined and live for months just on milk; sometimes I would eat as much as a great, holy pig. Sometimes I would meditate ten hours a day, sometimes I would dream about women and the pleasures of the world. I could not understand why it was happening, and I went through a lot of mental turmoil to examine why I was living in the cave. One day it dawned on me that the cave was good only to make me go through these shocks and find out whether I really cared for God or cared for God only because I was not able to cope with my insecurities and distractions. I had imagined, "If I could just realize God, I would be like Buddha or Jesus." We all go through these dreams, and the more we grow, the more we are able to dispel them.

It is good for our ego to believe we are concerned about God and spiritual freedom, but it is important to realize that we are just fooling ourselves. Let us examine some simple things that will demonstrate where we stand.

SELFLESSNESS

ALL RELIGIONS teach us to practice selflessness. But how many of us go out of our way to help and care for others? We feel so insecure about ourselves and so involved with our own safety that we don't have any time, energy, or money to spare for others. Sometimes we do, but that is only to fool ourselves that we are selfless, just as we meditate to fool ourselves that we are now reaching Divine consciousness. Get rid of these delusions. You are not in the least selfless. The day you are selfless is the day you will be enlightened and free. Fear makes you selfish. Self-ishness keeps you confused. Confusion makes you act as if you were selfless so you can imagine how wonderful you are.

We are inspired by Mother Teresa, St. Francis, Jesus, and Gandhi; we adore them and proclaim how great they are. What does it take to be great? Selflessness. If I could be selfless, I would not fear for the self. In the very process of self-lessness, I lose the self, I transcend the self, I dissolve the self and become the whole, big Self.

I don't believe in swamis, Ph.D.s and yogis; I just believe in plain, simple truths. Even if you are not a puritanical person, a disciplined person, an intelligent person, or a spiritually inclined person, you still can have a glimpse of that freedom. After such a glimpse, you will be 100 times better than any disciplined, puritanical, spiritually inclined person. Keep yourself open to that experience.

If you read the lives of great mystics who were God-realized, you find that they were just human beings like you and me. What is this freedom that they had? What is this freedom that we lack? I used to struggle for that freedom, but one day it dawned on me that "This is it." That realization changed my attitude toward life and toward others. Life was the same, but there was a difference in the quality of that life.

Suppose you believe you have to struggle to keep breathing in order to stay alive, and that if you don't make an effort every minute you will die. This belief will keep you tense and afraid. Suppose another person knows, "Breathing goes on whether I make an effort or not." How relaxed that person will be. Question yourself, "To what am I bound right now?" and see how your mind struggles with its own confusion. It neither can decide that it is free nor admit that it is bound. It keeps bouncing. Observe this confused bouncing between freedom and bondage. If you can recognize that you are free at least for this moment, then celebrate it. Have it. It is yours. If you feel you are worried and haunted, make that thought the center of your attention. See how long it bothers and frightens you. Even if you want to hold onto the thought, you cannot because you and the mind and the thought are unreal—changing—so how can you hold onto it? Either you are ready to work on this subtle plane of noticing yourself, or you are interested just in financial or emotional freedom, in which case don't confuse yourself with spiritual freedom.

ACKNOWLEDGE
WHERE
YOU ARE

THERE IS NOTHING wrong in looking for money and toys, but admit that that's where you are. If you have integrity on that level of consciousness, you will realize that freedom is spiritual. Divinity is the expression of integrity. Be there. Know you are a pig. Know you are fat and lazy. Know you are compulsive. Know you are attached. Mind cannot find fun anywhere but in God. It recognizes and appreciates God according to its level of consciousness. If you are interested in toys, be total and enjoy them. Gradually you will see that they make no sense, and you will move on. Don't build big concepts about being dutiful, loving, humanitarian, and busy with so many responsibilities. Who made you responsible, and for whom? See your attachments, fears, and tendencies, and work from where you are. If I am sitting in Ohio, can I work in New York?

If you start observing yourself, you will find that the problem of bondage is not because of your helplessness in having to work for a living and pay your bills. Nor is it because of your inertia that you goof off. It is mostly because of confusion. Goof off as much as you want, but before you goof off be sure of yourself. Develop clarity to get rid of confusion. If you can break your confusion just once, freedom will be there automatically, and your mind will feel inspired to meditate, to help others, and to enjoy serenity and well-being. Why do you feel good in meditation? Although you do not always feel high, you feel victorious that you have been faithful to your conviction. You celebrate yourself for doing your best according to that conviction.

Once a king killed a deer while it was having sexual intercourse with its partner. In reality, the deer was actually a seer who had mystical powers that allowed him to take on the appearance of a deer. Just as he was about to die, he appeared in human form and cursed the king. "As you have killed me while I was having intercourse, you also will die while having intercourse with your wife." The king knew that if he dared to have sex, he would die.

So he went home and told his wives that he was going to retire to the forest and live a holy life, that he was not interested in palaces or material things anymore. He did not tell them the real reason. The wives insisted on going with him to serve their husband in his new life. After a long time, one of the wives sweetly told him how wonderful he was, and he could not control himself. He had intercourse with that wife and died.

You are trying to tell yourself that one day you will rule yourself. You are never going to rule yourself completely, not even if something you are doing is injurious to you; but you can harmonize yourself, integrate yourself, and understand yourself. Then you can transcend yourself—not in the sense of being victorious over things, but in the sense of going beyond your ego. There is where you can realize the real freedom, joy, and beauty of life. When you are ready for divine freedom, it will come right away. Whatever freedom you experience right now is the freedom you are

145

ready for. It is not as if you are hungry but cannot have food. When you are spiritually hungry, you are provided spiritual food then and there.

———————————

LITTLE SPARKS

ONE SPARK OF fire can consume millions of trees. We are not trying to wipe out our precious forests, but making an analogy: The tiniest spark of wisdom, freedom, or love can consume your ego and reveal the overwhelming power of your Divine Essence. So if you have the tiniest spark of wisdom, freedom, or love, adore it; celebrate it; feel proud of it. Whether you recognize it or not, God is testing you by providing the tiniest spark of peace, the tiniest spark of love, the tiniest spark of freedom. Unless you learn to appreciate your little sparks of peace, love, and freedom, you will not be flooded with cosmic peace, love, and freedom. Try it. You will find that the more you appreciate that tiny spark, the more it will consume you and release you from your separate individuality. You may think you have only a tiny bit of wisdom and freedom, but this little spark can do the greatest miracle for you and all mankind. It always begins with a tiny spark.

———————————

LOOKING
FOR
FREEDOM

WHAT ARE YOU looking for? Are you looking for freedom? Or are you looking for amusement? Know your level of consciousness. If you are looking for a kick—through movies, your partner, money, or something else—let that be how you are right now. With patience, practice, and clarity, you will refine your taste. The more you practice according to your own understanding and appreciate your own clarity, the more you will feel a deeper and deeper sense of freedom. Only when you realize that you are in prison can you do something to get out.

What is freedom? Are you not free already? What do you need in order to experience freedom? It is in the awareness of awareness, in the awareness of being, that you experience freedom. Ultimately, you have to forget your money and partner to enjoy freedom. If you are constantly thinking about them, you are living in hell because you are carrying the burden of that thought. Recognize what makes you feel bound and see how long that source of bondage stays in the space of your consciousness. If you feel free, celebrate it. There is nothing to attain, nothing to achieve, nothing to prove. It's here and now. Relax in your own glory. All bondages and fears belong to your feelings. Awareness is always pure, like the sky.

In your night dreams, sometimes you go through hell. Perhaps you are trapped, or drowning. But when you awaken, do you worry that you are still trapped or drowning? Or do you think, "Thank God the dream is over"? Don't be like that crazy woman who saw a lion in her dream. When she awoke, she was still crying. Someone asked, "Why are you crying?"

She told him, "The lion is chasing me."

The man asked, "Where is the lion?"

She answered, "I have seen it, I have seen it!"

"When?" the man asked.

"When I was dreaming, I saw it with my own eyes."

"That was a dream. Where is the lion now?" he asked.

She kept repeating, "I have seen it, I have seen it; it can't be unreal."

When you dream, you can do nothing but dream; but when you awake, don't be confused that you still are dreaming. The dream is over, the pain is over. Who cares if, in a dream, you die one hundred times? When you awake, you find yourself intact. Similarly, when you are truly awake and alert, you find that your awareness is pure and whole. You don't need money or a home or anything to feel your wholeness. You already are that wholeness.

THE IMPORTANCE
OF
LOVE

YOUR LOVE IS important to everyone who comes into your life, and you are important in someone's life. When you treat yourself with the dignity of that awareness, you make yourself happy and make others happy too. When someone comes into your life, feel blessed that he or she has come. Don't feel you don't need anyone. That is nonsense. We all share this cosmic existence. If there is a thorn in my foot, do my eyes boast, "We don't care about the thorn, since it is only pricking the foot"? Everything is part of the unity. So when someone shows you a gesture of love, take it with openness and realize that this person has come into your life to say hello.

Freedom is not anywhere where it must be sought; it is within and without, always in the core of your being and in the core of every moment. Just put your attention there. Jesus smiled at water, and the water turned into wine. In the glory of your awareness, all bondage turns into freedom.

Mind is constantly seeking the freedom that is God. When mind is not ready to experience God or freedom in its pure form, it makes compromises—with a sweetheart, for example, or with objects of the world.

If you are not looking for enlightenment, there is nothing wrong with your consciousness. Don't condemn yourself and create this rift in your psyche. When you condemn yourself, you are condemning the Divine process itself. You become peaceful by hugging your child, by watching flowers, or walking by the ocean. Don't hesitate to appreciate yourself for that. You have hesitated enough; it is time to accept it, trust it, and appreciate it.

REALITY
AND
ILLUSION

WHEN WE USE the words "reality" and "the illusion of individuality," we have to be clear about what we mean. When we compare the term "reality" to the term "illusion," we mean that reality which will outlast any other form of appearance. All other forms of appearance that we consider real are not quite real in comparison to that reality.

When you stand in front of a mirror, you see your reflection. Your reflection is real; yet you know that when you turn your face away, the reflection vanishes. In comparison to your face, the reflection is unreal. When you dream, you experience pleasure and pain, success and failure; you interact with friends and enemies. Everything in the dream seems as real as everything in the waking state. Yet when you awaken from the dream, you find that the dream and dream experiences—including your dreaming self that was having the experiences—were an illusion. Everything was just your mental projection. If you are drowning in the dream, you wake to find that your body is intact and that the waking experience is more real than the dreaming experience. When you are in the dream state, you don't remember the waking state; you consider the experiences of the dream state to be normal and real. While you are in the dreaming state, you cannot deny or cancel the waking state; but when you return to the waking state, you can refute the dream state because you have a higher perspective.

Comparing these two states makes it easier to understand the higher form of reality beyond the dream state and waking state. This individual self that enables me to write these words to you and that enables you to read them seems real, but it is not absolutely real. There is a higher form of reality, which enables us to transcend the so-called reality from which currently relate to each other.

WHICH LIFE
IS
REAL?

WHAT CRITERIA confirm this to be a reality? And how can we be sure we really exist and are really relating to others? By observing the experiences you are having right now, can you conclude that this is reality? How can you say that the dream is not reality? Pleasure and pain are as real in the dream as in the waking state. Sometimes somebody kills you in a dream, but when you awaken you find yourself alive. Which is real? In waking life, you may be very ugly, poor, or unsuccessful; in the dream, you may appear to be very beautiful, successful, intelligent, and powerful. Which of the two is real?

This question has been raised from time immemorial, but most of us are not concerned about such questions. We are just concerned with having a good time or making a contribution to society as a speaker, a teacher, a writer, etc. Each of these is an expression of individuality, and most of us pass our lives in those pursuits. Ordinary individuals are not ready to question the core of individuality and ask, "Who am I?" They are so involved in pursuing the ambitions of this reality that they feel satisfied if they fulfill them. For others, this question has to arise in the process

154

of their unfoldment.

In Indian mythology, a king named Janaka had a dream in which he was bitten by a mad dog. Janaka wanted the doctor to treat him, but the doctor refused because the king did not have two rupees to pay the fee. In agony, the king awoke. He knew that nobody should disobey him; but when he was in pain in the dream, the doctor had refused to treat him. He wondered: was he the king who could order anyone in the kingdom to do anything, or was he just a poor, ordinary individual?

King Janaka gathered a big assembly of scholars, mystics, saints, and ascetics, and posed this question. There was one enlightened saint who resolved the riddle. He told them that neither of the two Janakas—neither the one in the waking state who was a king nor the one in the dreaming state who was bitten by a dog and looking for medicine—was the real Janaka. There was a third Janaka beyond these two.

155

INDIVIDUALITY
AND
SECURITY

IF YOU OBSERVE the lives of those who seem to be very happy, successful, and powerful, you will find that they are not perfectly content. Nothing obvious may be wrong with them; they may be virtuous, kind, and successful; but they have not realized the Essence beyond their individuality. Those who are more evolved see the delusion of security based on individuality. No matter how rich or powerful people may become, how wonderful a lover they have, or how beautiful they look, their pain, worry, and fear continue: "I may lose my power, my beauty, my vitality, and my lover." Whether we are good or bad, the urge to realize that Divine core, that universal reality and freedom from all worries and responsibilities, is inherent in each of us. Just as we don't have to create hunger or the desire to sleep, so we don't have to create the urge to realize freedom and be blissful.

When we question our individuality in a positive way, we become able to transcend it. Then we realize the reality that cannot be described through words. Words belong to the realm of names and forms, and reality is beyond names and forms. For example, when you sleep soundly, you know it, you like it, you miss it and feel miserable when you go without it—but can you describe it? The difficulty is in words. We can communicate experiences only if the other person has had the same experience. Here we are exploring something that is beyond language and mind. As long as mind is involved, I will be me, and you will be you; there will be a duality. When we experience the reality beyond duality—when we go to that higher dimension that transcends duality—our mind reveals something from within itself and realizes serenity, contentment, and joy. The experience is direct and transcendental.

How do you enjoy a cup of coffee? If there is joy mixed in that coffee, the more you drink the more you should feel joyful; but it doesn't work that way. After one or two cups, that's it. The same is true with movies, sex, food, drinking, anything. You usually experience joy through some medium or vehicle, but when it comes to experiencing joy within yourself, you don't know how to do that. As long as you experience joy through someone or something else, you remain dependent on that person, thing, or situation, so your quest for happiness and freedom will never be complete and fully satisfying.

No matter how successful you become, you will remain insecure as long as you live on the plane of individuality. Even if you have the most beautiful body and have been chosen Miss USA or Mr. Universe or received the Gold Medal at the Olympics and beaten your own world record, the question remains: How long can you hold onto that? Everything wears out. In the realm of individuality, our beauty, vitality, relationships, intelligence, power, and achievements all fizzle out. That is why an individual mind never feels secure. When we build our security on those things, it is not going to work, and mind is not trained to see the mirage. When you go to a movie, you enjoy it; but if you think you need to own the movie house, screen, and actors, there is something wrong with you—there is nothing there. Go and have a good time, but be ready to leave. All of our experiences are like movie experiences. When we are in this plane of individual consciousness, we want to settle in the movie house because the movie is so great.

SHARING
LOVE

G O BACK TO simple experiences. When you walk on the beach or watch a hummingbird or smell a flower, do you think of your failures and successes, your beauty or ugliness? You forget all that. You forget about your limited self and go beyond your personality into the realm of serenity. Whenever you are peaceful, you are not separated from other human beings or things of this world. Everything becomes part of everything. We all are seeking that serenity. We all experience it on and off, but somehow we are not ready to grasp it.

When you share your love—not only in an intimate human relationship, but even when you feed your child or your puppy and really enjoy seeing them eat—how do you enjoy that? If you are only your body, how can you be happy seeing someone else happy? Somehow you must be present in that person, in that puppy, in order to feel their happiness. That is the glory of love, and that is why there is so much emphasis on selfless love. If you are able to be happy when you see or make someone else happy, then you are able to transcend your limited, separate self. Because the Essence within this body is not confined to this body, what relates to the Essence can express joy somewhere else, and you will feel happy. It is through selfless love that you realize this higher dimension of consciousness.

It is a paradox. All your struggles are to hold onto something —"my house," "my garden," "my husband," "my country"—my … my … my. We don't want to share. Meditation is easy, prayer is easy, all the austerities are easy, but sharing is difficult. You may share occasionally to fool yourself how loving and selfless you are. But when real sharing takes place, you realize that it enhances your own glory, peace, and attunement, because by sharing you are transcending your limited body-consciousness. You are not losing anything by sharing. You are opening a higher dimension of consciousness for yourself in which you will transcend all your limitations. There will be no comparisons. I will become you, and you will become me. Then who will defeat whom? Who will hate whom? Who will be superior or inferior to whom?

We are all looking for the experience that happens whenever we are peaceful. We all experience the same peace, but through a different medium. Through selfless sharing or meditation, we reach that peace and experience that love without requiring any medium. Meister Eckhart said, "The eye with which I see God is the same eye with which God sees me." Jesus said, "I and my Father are one." Why do we feel inclined to believe Jesus, Moses, Krishna, St. Francis, or Mother Teresa? Because something is so powerful in their lives, in their joy, in their love and peace that we cannot resist it. We are part of that truth. You came from the same Source as they did. We all came from one Source, and we are all looking for that same Source of peace, love, joy, and freedom.

Imagine a huge tree. In that tree are thousands of flow-

160

ers and fruits, and millions of thorns. Each of the flowers and fruits has its individual consciousness, and all are comparing and competing with each other. A few thorns in the tree have lost their individual consciousness. They do not perceive themselves as separate thorns, good or bad. They think, "I am a unique expression of the tree." Try to experience the freedom and contentment of a thorn that sees itself as the whole tree. Then see the limitations, worries, and pressures of all the fruits and flowers, with their beautiful flavors and fragrances, that are insecure about constantly losing their beauty. The thorns are free from limited self-consciousness, while the flowers and fruits are still confined to their individuality. Do we all want to be like those fruits and flowers, or are some of us willing to be like the thorns and identify with the Source?

The sun remains the same. We can have millions of reflections of the sun through different mirrors and buckets of water, but these reflections cannot exist on their own without the sun. If you break the mirror or empty the bucket, the sun is unaffected and remains always shining in its own glory. Like the sun, you remain unchanged, unaffected in your Essence. Only your reflection, your individuality, goes through ups and downs. Pure consciousness keeps supporting you even when you go into inertia or unconsciousness. That is why after sound sleep you can say, "I was not aware of anything, while I slept, but I enjoyed it." How could you be aware of that enjoyment if you were not present? In that Essence, you are neither a woman nor a man, neither successful nor unsuccessful; you are not an American, and I am not an Indian. In that awareness, we all are one; we all are peaceful, content, and joyful.

So spare some time in your daily life to attend to your pure awareness, to attend to yourself as you know it. Learn to own your feelings and see how long a particular feeling stays in the space of your consciousness. Instead of reacting to your feelings, just wait and watch. See how long these clouds hover in the sky of your awareness. When they go, you will realize that you are just the sky. Be aware of your peacefulness and contentment. The more you become aware of your awareness and contentment, the more you will become convinced that it is your real nature. You cannot lose it even if you want to. You cannot kill God within you even if you want to. When you realize the truth, you become free.

On this physical plane, body and mind will keep going through ups and downs; but deep down, the Essence remains changeless. As Essence we all are the same. On the surface I am me, I am not you, my hand is not my foot, and my eyes are not my ears; but they belong to the same body unit, the same cosmic unit. All weaknesses are just fabrications of the mind. First, you have to be integrated. When you are integrated for yourself, then you can be integrated and faithful to your spouse, your children, and your community. Then your self is no longer limited. It is universal, Divine, filled with peace, love, light, and joy.

THE
BOOK OF LIFE

YOU ARE PULLED in totally opposite directions by two things that happen simultaneously in your life, which confuse you so much that you don't know where or who you are. One is the pull of your individuality, the core of your vanity and specialness. The other is the pull of your limitless, transcendental Essence. You do not know whether you want to be an individual entity struggling for superiority and money, or whether you want to get rid of yourself and merge into that being which is beyond your-self, and in which there is no sense of otherness.

Instruments
of
Service

IN THIS COUNTRY, your struggles are not primarily centered on survival and food, as in mine, but on your image, skills, and creativity. You feel that you have not done enough, that you still have more potential to bring forth.

When is it going to be enough?

It only becomes enough when you realize the higher dimension of life that is beyond individuality. Even if we don't meditate, each of us is connected with that. Just remember any simple incident of your life when you were loving and tender. The simple experience of feeling love and tenderness toward anyone indicates something beyond individuality. You are not merely this gross body, so whenever you express yourself in a dimension that is more than your body you glimpse your universality.

Each of us has been blessed with that sort of experience at one time or another. I remember asking my professor, "What do *you* get if I get a high mark? It is only I who will succeed and get appreciation. Why does it matter to you?"

He answered, "It just feels great."

We love to be instruments of service and sharing. Yet we know that in day-to-day life, we all are fighting the struggles of "me" and "mine"—"my car," "my house." But our few moments of universality are just enough to allow us to transcend our attachment to our possessions, to transcend our vanity. While each of us tries to prove how wonderful we are as an individual person, we are loving our children and friends in such a way that we are transcending our limitations. If being selfless, meditative, and disciplined makes you feel better about yourself, why don't you repeat these things? Handle each moment in light of your convictions.

What are your convictions? You can find out from your own book of life.

DISCOVERING
YOUR
CONVICTIONS

THE MOST uplifting and rewarding chapters in the book of your life are those in which you were being selfless or victorious over your own mind. It is better to live in hell and be victorious over your mind and compulsiveness than to live in heaven but be defeated by your own mind and negative tendencies.

I have a problem with my eating habits: I tend to overeat. So far, despite all my spiritual disciplines, I never have found my mind disciplined enough to tell me, "That's enough." It always says, "Yes, enjoy a little more." When I overeat, I feel bad about myself; I feel lethargic and dull. The paradox is that I can enjoy myself by overeating and suffer later, or I can accept a little pain of self-control in the beginning and later enjoy the sweetness of being healthy and in good shape.

Whether you are a doctor, an engineer, a swami, or an attorney, this type of problem faces you, and you have to make a choice. When you overeat, it makes you feel good at first—but later do you like the effect? When you over-drink, oversmoke, over-gamble or do anything beyond moderation, do you feel good about it? When you behave within your limit, even if you don't feel good about yourself in the beginning, later on you do. Your own experience suggests that you should lead a life of self-victory, moderation, and selflessness, a life that is conducive to your peace and health.

SURRENDERING
HAPPENS
ON ITS OWN

AS YOU FEEL hungry in the flow of life, you also feel the need to take care of this hunger. You don't have to read the Bible to know what to do when you are hungry. You don't have to pray to God, "Please awaken me if I continue to sleep." When the time is right to sleep, you feel sleepy, so you sleep. Then you just wake up. You trust life by observing that it is happening. Life presents itself moment by moment, and you move on with the realization that there is nothing to do but move on.

In the beginning, you may feel like trying to surrender; but when you really become expert in surrendering, you realize that surrendering is happening on its own. There is a gravitational force in the earth. Even if you don't know about it, it works on your body anyway. No matter where you run, you cannot run away from gravity. You may keep fighting without result, or relax and surrender.

We are so accustomed to doing. Even sitting idly is doing something. See what you are doing and go deeper with it. Many times you meditate to cover up your insecurities in the name of spirituality. Be honest with yourself, realize your weakness, and then see how you can put the light of your meditation to heal that wound, how you can use God in your life to heal that suffering, that scar in your heart. Once you are healed, there is nothing to worry about, lose, or fear. You become intoxicated, and there is nobody other than you, only so many pictures. It is as though you go into a building of mirrors and see so many of your own forms. You embrace yourself from all sides because there is no one other than yourself.

When you go into a crowd where everyone is celebrating, your individuality vanishes. Then you experience the vast multitude as if you are the multitude, the whole. Your self-consciousness merges in the consciousness of the crowd. Awareness of your self-consciousness leads to Cosmic Consciousness. The best thing that can happen in your life is to have your self-consciousness merge into the Cosmic Consciousness.

Individuality is like an ice cube. We can use it to have a cold drink, but somehow it starts melting when we mix it with water or juice. Our individuality, too, should know how to melt. Love your individuality, but be ready to melt.

When you pour water into your cup, the water takes the form of the cup. When you pour the same water onto a plate, the water takes the form of the plate. When you pour water into a glass, the water takes the form of the glass. Whatever you pour it into, water takes that form. When you are as flexible as water, you are letting God celebrate His or Her glory through you. But when you become very tight, your individuality of "this is me" gets in the way of Divine expression. Your flexibility, your adaptability, is the sign of Divine beauty, Divine creativity working through you.

You are here in this space. It looks like a room because there are walls that create the form of a room. But space is not concerned with the walls around it or within it.

Your reality is like space; your individuality is like a room. It looks to be in a particular form. But don't concentrate on the walls, the appearance of the form; concentrate on the space. It is space that makes your movements possible. Without space there can be no walls.

When you appreciate the space within yourself that accommodates all your thoughts and feelings—when you appreciate the light that reveals all your thoughts and feelings—you relate to yourself from a universal point of view. You realize that your light is not just your light: it is the same light shining through all eyes; it is the same consciousness pulsing through all hearts; it is the same joy glowing through all faces.

You know that your body is separate from my body or from your friend's body. You experience your own pleasures and pains. When you are hungry, only you are hungry; when you eat, only you are full. It is your individual experience. In your mind you have particular thoughts, which others don't share. There is nothing mystical about recognizing one's individuality through body, mind, thoughts, feelings, image, or ego; but "this is me" is not the ultimate reality.

INDIVIDUALITY
AND
DOING

YOU THINK THAT because you do certain things, you are the doer. This sense of doership is one method for holding onto the illusion of individuality. If you are a solid entity, if you really have an individuality, why don't you stick with your decisions? You pick one romantic partner today, next day you don't care for her or him. At night, you decide to get up early in the morning; but when morning comes, you don't. You decide that starting today you will not be jealous, but next day you return to the old pattern. If you act lovingly at one time, why don't you act that way again and again?

When you go deeper into this question, you realize there is no such individuality which is choosing this or that. Your body/mind complex is directed by certain tendencies that you have accumulated over many years or lifetimes. There are certain *gunas*, forces of nature, that are working through your body and mind. We call those gunas *sattvaguna* when you feel clear and attuned; *rajoguna* when you feel aggressive and ambitious; and *tamoguna* when you feel lethargic and dull. As seasons keep changing, so these gunas keep changing, and your body and mind act

171

differently because of these changing energies. Because you are not clear about these forces of nature nor in touch with the inherent tendencies that make you do certain things, you take credit for doing what you do.

Individuality is like a shadow: it is there, and you can see it, but at the same time it is not there. The reflection in the mirror is there, yet at the same time it is not there. You see its absence as well as its presence, and you become detached from yourself. Like a bubble in the ocean, no matter where you emerge, you are never without water, and no matter where you merge, you never merge into anything but water. You move freely, act freely, embrace everyone freely because you fear nothing and have nothing to lose or gain.

CELEBRATE

YOU AND I have to learn to celebrate much, much more. When you are doing your vacuum cleaning, you are doing your best at that moment. It is your ego that creates the fragmentation, "I should be going to church; I should be meditating; I should be ..." No, you are doing fine. If God is everywhere, God is in vacuum cleaning too. It is your attitude toward that particular action that is responsible for revealing or not revealing God for you. You are gradually forced to open yourself to that acceptance, that surrendering, that celebration.

If you open the book of your life, you will find many chapters scattered here and there filled with glowing moments of peace, love, joy, sharing, and trust. You can glimpse a higher dimension of consciousness by becoming aware of these simple, innocent moments. Whenever you are driving, remind yourself that you are doing great. Remember your focal point or some prayer, something that touches your heart and moves you. If you simply do things without being aware of doing them, you miss that dimension of awareness called enlightenment or self-realization. Do good things and be aware you are doing them.

Recognizing goodness is recognizing God within you in that situation. When these moments visit you, you will be overwhelmed, thrilled, and transported; but you have to be there to greet them. If you think it is egotistical to recognize something good about yourself, then you are not really ready to take off, and you will remain stuck. Life is inspiring you to take off into that dimension of freedom. There is a mystical nature to those moments. Even when you meet someone after a long time, you enjoy that same ecstasy. Try to catch these moments.

In the beginning, you cannot work in an abstract way, but you can have a focal point as an anchor for your mind. A focal point is that thought which you have chosen intentionally to remind you of your peace, your awareness, your aspiration. When you are not required to think something specific, you remember your focal point. When you need to think other thoughts, tell your focal point you are going; when you come back, report again. Large companies have a security system. You can't go out without getting clearance; when you come back, you again have to get clearance. Let your focal point work for you as a security system. Your focal point could be a rose, your breathing, the name of Jesus or Mary, something that clicks with your heart. Awareness of this simple focal point will inspire you.

DEVELOP
A
ROUTINE

WHEN YOU GO to your office, a particular outfit is required, you are due at a particular time, your appointments are for certain times. But when it comes to God, you take God for granted. If you can be punctual for the office, can't you have a fixed time for being with God? If you have a focal point and a routine, you are going to enjoy universal consciousness, and nothing can stand in your way.

Live one moment at a time and allow yourself to be absorbed in that sweet space of your own gentleness and calmness. There you will experience the space of universal love, light, and joy beyond your individuality. The greatest thing you can achieve is to transcend your individuality and realize the oneness of life. Once you reach that state of consciousness, you are free forever, you are fearless forever. You have no choice but to smile, you have no choice but to love, you have no choice but to surrender.

OPENING
YOUR HEART

WHEN WE BUY a lottery ticket, we believe in the lottery.
If we had as much faith in God's grace as in the lottery,
we would have all the faith we needed to receive Divine
grace. If you put a bottle with a tightly sealed cork into the
ocean, water will not get into the bottle. But if you remove
the cork and tip the bottle toward the ocean, water will get
into the bottle. Your heart is like that bottle. It must be open.
If you are not open, Divine grace cannot seep in and
saturate you.

Becoming helps you to realize your "being," but it never
guarantees that it will reveal your being. Even if you have
become nothing and achieved nothing, you can be in touch
with your being. One person may have become what he
wanted to become but not be in touch with his real being.
Someone else may not become what he wants to become,
yet be himself and in touch with his being. We may relate
to being and have glimpses of being, yet not recognize and
catch it. For a moment, now, remember a life experience
that was very peaceful, thrilling, or satisfying for you. Try
to relate to your being at that moment. Being is freedom,
and freedom means celebration of being.

Because of our attachment to pleasures, we think, "When I become free, I will have a good time." It is sheer ignorance to think that way. Freedom means you don't fear pain. You can share, endure, challenge, and transcend the pain of poverty, sickness, loneliness, jealousy, hatred, and so on. We need to realize that pain is simply a fact of life. The more we fear it, the more we increase it. The more we challenge it, the more we transcend it. Get in touch with your pain. Pin it down. What is it that's pinching you?

LOVING BEING

THERE ARE FOUR basic needs of life.
First is health. Whether we believe in God or not, we all want to be healthy. Even to enjoy pleasures, we have to have good health.

Second is money. We want to eat, we want a house, we want clothes, we want a car. These require money.

Third is relationships. If nobody loves me, and I love nobody, I feel lonely. No one wants to be ignored and neglected. We all want to be loved. As my body needs food, so my mind needs love, recognition and appreciation. The first three categories belong to the realm of becoming

Fourth is attunement, getting in touch with being. The fourth category belongs to the realm of being. Being loved for anything other than being involves inevitable loss. Whoever is supporting me will someday die. Every day, I lose some of my youth and vitality. So the person who loves me only for those qualities is not going to love me if I keep losing them. The mind likes to think, "That person loves me for my being," but this is nonsense. Someone loves you because there is something lovable about you. You may be sweet, beautiful, rich, talented, or compassionate, but the moment you lose that particular quality the person's love will fade. The day you are able to love someone just for his or her being—the moment you are able to love being—personality fizzles out.

It is all one everywhere. Your being is not separate from her being; her being is not separate from his being or my being. So who is loving whom? When you reach that dimension of being, you can do nothing but love because you *are* love. The more you are in touch with your being, the more you exude love. You don't have to do anything. It is automatic.

No matter what you become in the realm of becoming, unless and until you are in touch with your being, you can never feel secure. No matter what you have achieved in life, when it is time to die you cannot feel fulfillment unless you have experienced your being. If you have not been in touch with your being, you will die feeling you did not really achieve what you wanted to achieve. You did not know your Self, the knower of everything. It is good that you do not feel fulfilled, because that inspires and goads you to seek the Divine, to seek the Essence of life.

APPRECIATE
THIS
MOMENT

WHAT ARE YOU expecting from yourself? What do you want to become? What should you become to be yourself? Are you not already your self?

The energy you put toward becoming is so intense that it leaves nothing over for being. You are that being right now; but if your mind is involved with becoming something in an hour, a day, or a year, you will not appreciate this moment. To explore your relationship with the moment, tune into it and celebrate yourself for being as you are.

A RESTING PLACE
FOR
THE MIND

YOU HAVE A garage for your car, a closet for your clothes, a shelf for your books, and a bedroom for resting. Do you have a resting place for your mind?

If you don't have a resting place for your mind, can you complain that your mind is not peaceful and centered? All the experiences of life filter through the mind. You cannot appreciate your spouse, your car, your friends, or anything without the help of your mind. Everything reaches you through your mind, yet you ignore your mind.

FIND
A
FOCAL POINT

A FOCAL POINT IS a resting place for the mind. My focal point may be a mantra, while yours may be breathing. I may focus on the awareness of awareness, while you may focus on the image of Jesus or Mary. I may use Niagara Falls as a focal point, while you may focus on a sense of, "I am who I am."

I love Niagara Falls. I am so picky about whom to love and whom to trust, yet this enormous body of water falls without concern. Every second it lands: Boom ... Boom ... Boom. I want to become so intoxicated with my love that every second of my existence I have the experience of Love ... Love ... Love. Boom ... Boom ... Boom.

When you have nothing to plan and think, recognize that you are finished with thinking. This is the time for your mind to rest. To let your mind rest, visualize a focal point. Unless you do that, how can you get in touch with your being and not remain distracted and scattered with becoming?

First, convince yourself of the need for a focal point. Second, choose a focal point. Third, attune to the focal point by maintaining awareness of it whenever you are not thinking or planning. And finally, appreciate yourself for being in attunement with that focal point. When you remember a beautiful moment or object, you enjoy it again, so choose a focal point that is beautiful for you—and whenever you remember it, celebrate.

LIVING
WITHOUT
DIAPERS

YOU THINK THAT you do. You have created your self-image on the basis of this doing. But if you could understand that you never did, never do, and never will do anything, you would realize the being that is free from your image and becoming. The concept of free will, self-improvement, and becoming is strong in you because you don't trust yourself. Unless you observe and trust the process of the unfoldment of life, you may become an adult wearing beautiful jeans, but you will not be rid of your diapers. If you could see that there is no need for a diaper now that you are an adult, you would celebrate your adulthood and be free of your diaper. People such as Krishna, Jesus, Buddha, St. Francis, and Meister Eckhardt are very few. They were without diapers.

You think that if you do not control yourself you may not behave the way you should. You are on guard against yourself. Your mind knows that whenever you hurt someone knowingly or unknowingly, you are also hurt. Do you have to keep telling yourself not to stand in front of an oncoming car? In the course of life, your body and mind learn how to eat, how to behave, how to be loving and kind, how to be attuned. If these are happening in the flow of life, why are you creating this burden that you have to *do* them?

TRUSTING
THE
LIFE FORCE

THERE WAS ONCE a traveler on a train. He had never traveled on a train before, and he was carrying his luggage on his head. Someone asked him why. The man said, "This is the first time I have had the privilege of riding on a train. I know the train can carry my weight, but I don't know if the train can carry the extra weight of my luggage."

You are carrying your burdens on your head because you don't trust the Life Force. The moment you trust, you are free.

The more you let go of achievements and attainments that are in the realm of becoming, the more you enjoy freedom as pure being. You are that being which is supporting the whole paraphernalia of becoming. No matter what you become, you cannot become being. No matter what you cannot become, you already are being.

See the fullness of being. When you have love in your heart for your dog or your child, do you think, "I am not feeling the great love that Mother Teresa feels or Jesus felt"? It doesn't matter how rich or poor, beautiful or ugly, intelligent or dumb you are. The feeling of love is pure feeling.

Do whatever you do as well as you can. When you do it

186

as well as you can, you automatically are released from the sense of doing it. In the beginning, you are a doer, so try to be the best doer. When you are hopeless and compulsive, accept that role too. When that fizzles out, be the best doer again and see how you do what you do. When you are able to understand how you do what you do, you will realize that you really are not doing it—it is just happening. In the process of life, you feel hungry; in the process of life, you eat. In the process of life, you feel sleepy; in the process of life, you fall asleep. In the process of life, you learn that making others happy provides you great joy.

It is not a discipline to enjoy a movie. It is not a discipline to love. It is a burden if you have to love because you "should" love. Love is enjoying an expansion of yourself. Being kind, sweet, and loving are just expressions of your awareness. Some people are not able to trust that.

When you trust yourself, it means you trust the Life Force that is working through you. When your ego comes in, you think, "I have to achieve something. I have to become something," but the Life Force in you was bound to become what you have become and is bound to become what you will become. Don't confuse it with determinism. The Life Force is absolute in itself and expresses itself through each one of us. The more you trust yourself and approach life freely, the more you see the effulgence of being shining everywhere.

KNOWING
YOUR
DIVINE ESSENCE

I AM DIVINE, and I try to remind my friends that they are Divine, in the sense that there is a Divine process going on behind all our experiences, all our troubles, all our fears and fantasies. In that Divine process, we experience higher and higher truths, more and more profound and beautiful settings. It is just a normal blossoming. When we don't see that process rightly, we dislike ourselves or others; we judge ourselves or others.

SEEING
LIFE
IMPERSONALLY

ONCE WE CAN see the process that is going on, we see life in an impersonal way. As long as we take things in a personal way, our individuality or ego—which fears, judges, and compares—will get in the way. If we could ask a flower, "What makes you so beautiful, fragrant, and alive?" the flower would respond, "I am enjoying the experience of being beautiful, fragrant, and alive, but I am really doing nothing." It is a very difficult concept to realize that life is blossoming on its own and has an intrinsic force. To realize that, we have to reach a higher truth.

When you are dreaming, you take credit for doing what you do in the dream; but when you awaken you realize that the dream was just going on and that you were a product of it and just flowed with it. In the dream, somebody may have been deceitful and hurting or sweet and kind, but when you awaken you know there was no "somebody"; it was only you, manifesting in the form of friends and enemies.

Think of someone whom you consider hopeless or whom you hate. If you were to ask that person in a gentle, objective way, "What are you seeking?" that person would

189

tell you, "I am seeking freedom, beauty, love, light, and joy." When it comes to our real search, our real aspiration, there is no difference among us. Whether we are good or bad on the surface, we all seek the same thing. We all feel hungry, we all feel cold, we all crave water, and, because we come from the same Divine Source, we all are seeking That. Try to see that no matter how bad you think you are, it is just a passing phase of your divine unfoldment.

It is like the first time a woman is pregnant and looks in the mirror. She thinks, "How hopeless I am, how ugly I am; I used to charm my beloved with my beauty, but now I may lose it and him because I am not the same." That doesn't make sense; her huge belly has something very tender within it. In spite of our failures, we have the tenderness of Divine fulfillment, Divine success, and Divine understanding within us.

REAL
SUCCESS

ON WHAT BASIS do you consider yourself successful or unsuccessful? You consider yourself successful if you get a good job, if you can charm someone, if you get a better house, if your children get a good education. You get so carried away with your mundane comparisons that you lose sight of your ultimate goal, ultimate growth. Ask yourself, "What is the form of ultimate success?" If you can feel the answer, you can feel the essence of the success that you are seeking, and in that context you can decide whether you are successful or not.

Philosophically, if your mind is remembering your watch or your friends, how can you enjoy the fullness of your own being? Is it your ultimate goal to always be carrying so many thoughts? If that is your ultimate goal, you have to be even smarter and decide which wallet, watch, or person you want to think of constantly.

Psychologically, you care for a thing only because it can bring you back to yourself. We care for each other only as long as we are able to feel our own core of being. If you keep me away from myself, I may love you for some time, but then I am going to hate you because I will feel drained and dependent. Something will be missing in my life. The joy of life comes when we are brought back to our own core of being. Real success occurs when I am me, when you are you. The experiences we go through are simply unavoidable ups and downs in the flow of life, like waves in a mighty ocean. They come and go.

Your suit is not your body. It is good for the body; it protects the body; it may make the body look beautiful; but it is not the body. In the same way, all failures and successes are not really you. When you look at things with that higher perspective, then you just flow with the flow of life without feeling burdened or judgmental.

One of my friends asked me, "Is God here and now, or do we have to find Him somewhere else in some other time?"

I replied, "What do you think?"

He said, "I think it is both ways. Psychologically, I feel as though God must be somewhere away from me because I do not always feel peace, bliss, and selfless love; sometimes I feel lonely, jealous, fearful, or distracted. In a deeper sense, I reason that if there is really something like God, God must be everywhere, in hard times, in hard places, in all situations, in all people. So how can I divide myself from that universal presence of God? How can I be separate?"

We have to see it from both angles. Psychologically, you feel separated; but philosophically, when you open your heart to that higher Truth, your mind starts merging into that higher Truth like your dreaming self merges into your awakened self. As the dreamer, you seem to be far away from your bed. When you awaken, you realize, "I was dreaming. Here is my bed and my beautiful partner." In a psychological sense, we are far, far away from God, from Divine Essence; but in a philosophical sense, we have to realize we are there in that Divine lap, and we are nothing other than that same Divine energy. There is no Shantanand, no Jack, no Jim, no Ann. My tongue, my fingers, my toes don't have their own individuality. In a dream there are different people, but those people do not have their own independent individuality.

We all have convictions: "I should eat this way, I should not smoke, I should not drink, I should not fool around, I should meditate every day, I should be studying. Since I am not doing all these things, I am hopeless. Poor me." If, while you play that recording in your heart of "poor me," you meet someone, do you think that person will want to be with you? He will wonder if perhaps *he* is the poor one for having you fall into his life. When you make yourself a poor thing, you attract a poor person who does not have a healthy, powerful image of himself or herself and who is not transparent with love, peace, and acceptance. You have built many negative convictions around yourself, and the purpose of spiritual life is to break all these convictions, because they are utterly false.

INTEGRITY

WHEN WE SEE things clearly, we develop a sense of integrity. If we have a low self-image, we don't have a sense of integrity.

I have tried many hard things in my life. Let me tell you very humbly that I have failed, so now I have started trying the easiest things. Still I fail sometimes, but it doesn't matter. What do I want to prove? What do I want to experience? If I became Jesus or Moses, would the world not continue to die as it is dying? It is a process. The river is constantly flowing to the ocean. That does not mean we should not have canals and use water for irrigation. Life and death are part of that universal flow. We should all try our best to be great like Mother Teresa, Jesus, or Moses, but there is nothing wrong in being ourselves.

NUMBER
ONE
PRIORITY

To ACCEPT yourself with that openness, you have to
develop a sense of integrity. And you can develop that
integrity only when you have clarity about your priorities.
Is your number one priority your health, or relationships,
or money, or attunement through meditation? "Number
one priority" means you give your maximum time, maximum energy, maximum money in that one direction. Only
when you feel you have been faithful to this number one
priority will you feel a zeal in your life and have a sense of
integrity.

We all want to have a lover who is faithful—but we are
cheating each other and even ourselves. We decide to
meditate, but do we meditate? We decide not to be lazy,
compulsive, or scattered, but do we control that? When we
have this fragmentation within ourselves, how can we be
happy? If I am not happy with myself, how can you make
me happy? It takes time to see that my unhappiness stems
from myself and not from you. We love to blame others as
the source of our unhappiness because that is how we feel
good about ourselves. But when we go deeper, we realize
that no one in the whole world can make us happy or

unhappy. It depends on our own integrity.

You are Divine Essence, and Divine Essence is everywhere. If you give something to one hand and feel hurt because your other hand did not receive, you are a fool. You are expressing yourself here through this hand, there through that hand; that is how you enjoy your wholeness. You have to realize that it is all one in you—good, bad, beautiful, ugly, great, small—everything.

Let's not become too serious. I think the purpose of life is to be play-full and joy-full. Sometimes your mind acts foolishly, sometimes wisely, sometimes compulsively, sometimes discreetly. When you accept all the phases of life, you can afford to play and celebrate.

———————

DEDICATION

WE HAVE TO consider the complications and pressures that are working through this personality or individual consciousness. If God is your number one priority, meditate as much as you can. See how important mundane relationships have become in comparison to Divine attunement, and how much value we give to money. If I lose a hundred dollars, I can't forget it for days; but if I forget God, who cares?

DEVELOPING
DETACHMENT

IT IS ONLY IN a higher dimension of attunement and growth that we develop detachment. I used to be very attached to my toys, but when I got something better, automatically I gave them up. At this stage of consciousness we are holding onto material things. We pretend to be holy, but we know we are holding on.

If you feel high from success and depressed from failure, find something to which you can really be dedicated. We are seldom dedicated. Those whom we consider great men and women were dedicated to something. Some were dedicated to music, some to tennis, some to meditation. Through dedication you develop zeal and bliss. Through that dedication you transcend the sense of failure and success. When you become dedicated, it doesn't matter whether you succeed or fail; you just have fun being dedicated.

———————————

OFFERINGS
TO
YOUR BELOVED

DEDICATION reveals the Divine Essence and Divine process that is unfolding through you. When you have nothing to do, attend to your focal point. It is a symbol of your pure awareness and love. Gradually, mind will feel at ease and at home with that symbol. Spiritual training is building awareness of this focal point so the mind becomes more relaxed, more attuned. Ultimately, being aware of your focal point and love is the way to become more secure, more loving, more lighthearted and free.

Since we cannot get in touch directly with pure love and awareness, and since it is difficult to relate to abstract universal consciousness, we choose a symbol. If you have an altar or picture and offer a little incense or some flowers, you feel as if you have offered something to your Beloved, the Lord.

One more practical suggestion: Every day, have four or five minutes for meditation. Take these four minutes very, very seriously. Remember that these four minutes have two hundred forty seconds, and approach this with total seriousness as a huge amount of time. Celebrate each and every second with a sense of freedom. Usually, you are rushing, so convince yourself that you can afford to have these four minutes without thinking of where you have to go or what you have to do or become.

In those four minutes, have one minute for relaxing and enjoying restfulness. Don't think about God or your job or relationships. Imagine you have total retirement for one minute. Be total. Enjoy yourself. Take a break from brooding and fantasizing. Even if your mind can't help thinking, don't voluntarily think or brood. If involuntary thoughts come, let them come and go, as clouds come and go. Be restful.

Take two of your four minutes for your mantra, your breathing, your awareness, or whatever your focal point is. Bring your mind to your focal point and let your mind be saturated with that as if you, your mind, and your focal point are one. If you are meditating on Niagara Falls, become Niagara Falls.

And for the last minute, visualize your ultimate fantasy materialized. Visualize that you have achieved what you wanted to achieve, you have done what you wanted to do, you have become what you wanted to become. Now, notice that when you have achieved everything, done everything, and become what you wanted to become, you have become yourself. You are utterly fulfilled and content. Your Self is not conscious of any achievement, any action, any possession. It is enjoying profound contentment and peace.

In *The Tao of Physics,* author Fritjof Capra mentions that scientists can measure the movement of particles in one millionth of a second. Can you visualize a millionth of a second? Try it. It will take you only a millionth of a second. When I tried to visualize this, I found it impossible. There was no more time; I had reached a dimension where I was in touch with my "being," and it was like being on the edge of eternity. Can you visualize eternity? If you are fully in this moment, you are in eternity. If you try this, you will find you are in touch with your being. There is no struggle, no jealousy, no rivalry, nothing—just the peace of being, as if everything is there for you, eternally arranged and beautiful.

THE LOGICAL
AND THE SPIRITUAL
APPROACH

IT IS THE NATURE of the mind to label things. Labeling is meant to make things easy in our day-to-day life, but in the process of labeling, things sometimes become more complicated.

I have two hands. One I call "right," the other I call "left." Unless I give them these different names, you will have difficulty understanding which one I am talking about. So it helps to know this is left, this is right.

If I favor one hand at the expense of the other, I may be showing special love and appreciation for one, but I am hurting the whole body, and the hand that I want to show special favor is also ultimately hurt. By realizing pure is-ness, you realize the oneness of being that goes beyond the realm of East and West. My hands are separate and different from each other, but the Life Force is the same for both of them.

Two approaches work simultaneously in life. One is the logical approach, and the other is the spiritual. The logical approach creates divisions, distinctions, and categories and wants to reinforce those divisions and categories. The spiritual approach focuses on the fundamental unity or principle that goes beyond all divisions, distinctions, religions, and differences.

It is very difficult for the logical mind to appreciate the attitude of the spiritual mind. "Love thy neighbor as thyself" is an example. Here is yourself: this is your body, this is your mind, these are your pleasures, comforts, and ambitions. Why should you share with someone? You have struggled to make it in society—why should you be a sucker? How can you be both wise and a sucker? This is a problem that ordinary human beings face.

When we are evolved, we don't see it that way. When we are loving and giving, we do not see ourselves as suckers but realize the joy and beauty of a higher dimension of life. When you love your child, are you a sucker?

When your approach is influenced by the logical attitude, you create barriers of nationality or religion. This is good for our growth if it makes us united in feeling that we are citizens of one country: people find a common purpose, a common bond and zeal to put their efforts in one direction and share the effects of their common endeavor.

But as isolated beings, we can achieve nothing. The cloth of my shirt has been produced and sewn by somebody else. The car you drive was made somewhere and delivered by somebody else. We are interdependent, and we cannot survive as isolated beings; yet if we don't have a little touch of independence and self-responsibility, we don't learn how to become part of the whole. You have to accept yourself as an isolated being to take care of your food, exercise, attunement, and day-to-day needs. But if you keep thinking only in those isolated terms, then there is no relationship with you, your friends, your children, and other human beings; there is a sense of loneliness. Those who suffer from loneliness are those who have not been able to expand their hearts and consciousness through selfless acts. In those acts blossom the beauty of the soul, the richness of life.

We have to be responsible individually, but to make our life joyful and purposeful, we have to be loving and caring. Otherwise why live? If I don't trust you, or you don't trust me, we are always fearful and standing apart because you may hurt me or I may hurt you. The element of trust is a must, and trust comes when we break our barriers. With that understanding, we can explore the basic differences and similarities between East and West.

———————————

PURITY AND SIN

THE FIRST difference that comes to mind is the concept of sin or guilt on one hand and Divine purity on the other. In the Eastern approach, there is not much recognition of sin. In the Western approach, there is more emphasis on sin. When you recognize a sin, you take on the burden of guilt. In the East, we are taught that everyone is Divine, and that, one way or another, everyone is trying his or her best to realize that Divinity. As a bud naturally blossoms into a flower, so it is natural for each soul to blossom into the Divine effulgence of beauty, love, and joy.

In general, the East does not recognize that a person can go off the track and end up in hell. For the East, hell is not something permanent. Even if you go a little astray and find yourself in some imaginary hell or heaven, you cannot stay there permanently. The only place you can stay permanently is the Divine abode, which is meant for everyone.

This is a very liberal approach. It does not say that only if you are very pure, holy, and disciplined will you end up in that Divine abode or be blessed with liberation. Rather, it implies that every drop ultimately reaches the ocean. One body of water may be very pure, while another may be very dirty; but when water follows its course, it must meet the ocean. Since every soul is looking for happiness, and since happiness is really nowhere except in Divine Essence, every soul has to realize ultimately that it has been distracted. Then every soul has to retrace its steps so it can reach that Source of happiness which is both divine and universal.

INTERNAL
AND
EXTERNAL

T HE EASTERN approach is more internal, the Western
more external. The criteria of success or progress in the
West are external: what you can do with your hands, how
you can help others, how you can discover new things, how
you can learn and grow externally. The criteria of success
or progress in the East are internal: They emphasize peace,
attunement, equanimity, contentment, and self-acceptance. The emphasis is more on meditation and contemplation. The Western approach is geared toward external
actions; it puts more emphasis on selfless service and
actions concerning the advancement of daily life.

If you compare the lifestyle of monks here in the West
to those in the East, you can see that in the East they are
following their course as they are directed and inspired.
Their path is more of contemplation and meditation. Their
time is spent in chanting, meditating, and repeating God's
name. In the West, they also pray, meditate, and chant; but
the overall emphasis is to teach, to take care of the elderly,
and to do things for the welfare of society. Here the emphasis is on action; in the East, it is more on contemplation.

BEING
AND
THINKING

YOU MIGHT HAVE heard how Descartes said, "I think,
therefore I am." That is a Western approach. The Eastern approach is, "I don't have to think in order to be. First
and foremost, I am. That is the beginning." That is the basic
criterion. You cannot prove by any means that you are, and
you don't have to think in order to prove it. You are.
Thinking about where you are, how you are, and why you
are come later. The sense of is-ness is fundamental. In India,
they use the word *swayamsiddha*, which means self-evident. Your existence is self-evident.

I know that I am. I am aware of my being through my
mind; but when I'm not aware of my existence through my
mind, do I cease to exist? Suppose my mind is distracted
about paying the bills or driving the car; do I cease to be?
Whether I am aware of myself or not aware of myself, I
continue to be. That means the mind is not the determining
factor of my being. My being is free and independent of my
thinking, of my surface awareness.

In spiritual disciplines and practices, we try to build this
awareness of being—not by repeating the words, "I am, I
am," but by *experiencing* that I am. When we build this

awareness of I-am-ness, we realize that this I-am-ness has contentment, peace, and joy inherent in it. In the beginning, it is simply a concept, a sort of mechanical repetition; but when your mind merges in the core of your being, it realizes its own nature in the form of that contentment, peace, love, and joy.

That is called a "mystical" experience. It is called mystical because you are no longer limited to body-consciousness of, "I am an Indian, I am a man." When you are in touch with your pure being, you experience that your pure being is not Indian, not man, not woman. Your is-ness is free of all these distinctions and categories. We call the experience mystical because it gives you the experience of oneness with the whole.

———————————

THE FULLNESS
OF
THOUGHTLESSNESS

WHEN DO YOU feel at your best? If you could remember those experiences when you really felt your best, you would realize that although the setting was beautiful, the person was pleasant, and your health was good, you were not in touch with your body or friend or the setting. Somehow you transcended all that. When you transcended your body, partner, and situation, you got in touch with your being. That impact on you was so powerful that it left a deep imprint on your psyche. Whenever you enjoy anything—whether it is a movie, a cup of tea or playing with your children—you enjoy that moment because you go beyond thought.

We are constantly perpetuating our thinking process. Those who are more evolved don't want to perpetuate thinking because they know that thinking is a vicious circle leading nowhere. I would rather enjoy the space of thoughtlessness, peace, and joy than continue straining myself to think. It takes time, effort, and growth to recognize the fullness of thoughtlessness.

There are three states: inertia, thinking, and thoughtlessness. Thoughtlessness is not inertia; it is peace. In inertia, you are not aware of peace; your mind has lost its normal awareness in unconsciousness. In thinking, your mind is distracted by thoughts about guilt, what you have done in the past, or what you are going to do in the future.

If you observe the nature of the mind, it can't stay in the moment, because when it stays focused in the moment, it starts merging. When your mind starts merging, it experiences peace, which is beyond thought, and you are aware of an inner contentment and fullness. You are aware of being, which lacks nothing.

Heart and Mind

IN THE WESTERN approach, the mind is more powerful—too powerful. The thinking, bouncing, calculating mind has been given too much importance. Westerners, in general, are not ready to accept anything that does not filter through their reasoning. They have to be convinced. The Eastern approach is more through the heart. This does not mean that love is missing here or that intellect is missing there; it is just a difference in emphasis. Because the mind is more doubting and restless than the heart, where mind is emphasized it is difficult to meditate, believe, and trust. Unless the mind realizes the beauty of mindlessness, it keeps on repeating the same patterns.

How can you trust yourself or someone you love? The nature of mind is to doubt. "I am rich, but my heart may fail tomorrow; there may be nuclear warfare soon; I may lose all my money." No matter how secure you are on the surface, if you have developed a doubting mind, it can never really relax and feel at ease because of that attitude.

Yet you can always find people who are very peaceful and joyful. This is not because of external situations. They may be poorer than you and I and not raised in a comfortable way, but somehow they have developed an attitude of trust in the Divine flow of life.

I am reminded of the great words of Jesus, "Follow me. Let the dead bury their dead." It means, "Develop your heart. If you know me, how long are you going to mistrust? How long are you going to doubt?" You have to open yourself one day. That's how we receive God's grace— through trust and openness. As long as we over-emphasize the nature of mind that mistrusts and doubts, we never reach the dimension of grace.

The same thing is happening in day-to-day life. You go out with someone, but you don't trust. The problem is not that you don't trust the other person, but that you don't trust yourself. Those who have a problem trusting others really have a problem trusting themselves. It takes a lot of training, understanding, and growth to realize that the reason why you are not able to trust others is because you don't trust yourself. In your childhood you may not have received enough loving support and confidence; somehow, something got messed up, so you don't trust yourself now.

SHARING
AND
FREEDOM

THE EASTERN approach emphasizes much more loving interaction and mutual dependence. The Western approach emphasizes freedom more.

In the East, the emphasis is on love. Parents love to be with their children. Children are trained to feel blessed if they can serve their parents. In the West, the training is different.

In the East, we can become too attached. Parents live for the sake of their children. They cannot spend money, they cannot be at ease because they are always concerned about their children. It is almost a sickness in them. On the other hand, in the East there is a better understanding among family members because there is more emphasis on love and sharing, while in the West more emphasis is put on freedom: "My apartment, my bank balance, my car; mind your own business; leave me alone."

The problem we face in the West is the problem of loneliness. Freedom is good only when you have been able to expand your heart and consciousness. Just the freedom of not having to deal with anyone because you have plenty of money and your own car does not satisfy your heart.

Your heart needs some relationships. Your heart cannot be satisfied only with freedom unless and until you are very, very evolved and have gone through all the processes of relationships, love, and growth. Here, people suffer from loneliness because of the emphasis on freedom, but when too much emphasis is on money, you become attached to money and are no longer free. Money can buy only things, not freedom.

Because the East is not so rich, there is more mutual dependence: "I need you and you need me." Since we are somehow forced to need each other, we develop feelings and love for each other. That makes life more enjoyable and uplifting. In the West, there is more freedom of choice about life than in the East; but in philosophical and religious terms, the East offers more freedom. In the East, you can believe in God or not believe in God and still be considered a very good, very evolved person. Buddha himself did not talk about God. According to our Eastern orthodox approach, Buddha was considered an atheist. Someone who did not believe in the holy scriptures called *Vedas* was considered an atheist. In that light, Mahavir, another great Jain saint and Buddha were both considered atheists. Yet in spite of being considered atheists, they were considered evolved and enlightened. So there is much more freedom in spiritual approaches in the East.

Life in the East is dull. Everybody behaves, follows, and dresses according to almost the same orthodox pattern. In the West, you can have your own original thinking and not have to accept whatever someone has told you.

In the West, if you do not follow an evangelic approach or you are not a born-again Christian, you are considered by some to be lost. In the East, there is no such thing as being lost. You can believe in any deity, any form; you may or may not believe in God; yet you can be an enlightened person. In that sense, there is absolute freedom when it comes to a spiritual or philosophical approach.

———————————

ACCEPTANCE
AND
PERFECTION

IN THE WESTERN lifestyle, you may date someone, go out and eat anything; but in the East, you will not find that freedom. In that sense, the East is more orthodox, more rigid.

In the West, you find more emphasis on purity, on the approach of being a perfectionist. Since the West believes in sin, it also believes that everybody must be sin-less. This approach of sinlessness turns you into a perfectionist. You are always fighting against yourself: "Damn it, I still have anger, jealousy, lust; I still get drunk, I'm still lazy." The Western approach engenders more self-condemnation and fighting with oneself.

In the East, there is more ease about self-acceptance. There is no such craziness about being a perfectionist. It's all right to be lazy; it's no big deal. It's all right to lose your temper; also no big deal. Those things that are considered a big deal are because of social reasons, not because of philosophical or spiritual reasons. In the East, we are encouraged to accept ourselves as we are. No matter how we are, we are unique expressions of the Divine.

SEER AND DOER

SINCE THE WEST emphasizes action more, the approach is one of doing. You know yourself as a doer: you can accomplish things, prove things, change things; you are the author of your destiny. In the East, the approach is one of seeing. You watch, you flow with the flow of life, you bless things and situations, you are never affected by events; you are full and content within yourself by yourself. You are like light. If all of us continue to sit in this room, the light continues to give light; if all of us leave the room, it keeps giving light. It is not affected by our presence or actions.

Your real Essence is like the surface of a mirror. A mirror is never judgmental about your beauty or ugliness. It accepts you the way you are. If you are cranky or your breath is bad, your devoted husband or wife may not be loving and accepting, but no matter how you look or how you are, the mirror reveals you. Pure consciousness is like a mirror that reveals whatever goes through your mind, yet never is affected by what is revealed. Because of lack of understanding, we identify with our thinking, feeling, and calculating mind rather than with that pure light that reveals the different states of mind. The more you are in touch with your real Self, the more you identify with yourself as seer, as awareness that is not affected by the highs and lows of the mind, just as a mirror is never affected by beauty or ugliness.

The overall emphasis in the East is more on the seer, but the western mystics have not neglected this approach. As Meister Eckhardt said, "I pray to God to rid myself of God." Or take the powerful statement of Jesus, "Open your eyes and see, fields are shining for harvest." You don't have to do anything. It is already happening.

When you feel this light of pure awareness, you will be doing the same thing you did before—but now your attitude will be different. In the past, you were concerned that you had to do something: "I have to carry my shadow." Once you have the attitude of a seer, you know that even if you don't carry your shadow, your shadow follows you anyway. It is a difference in attitude. When we think that we are responsible for whatever we are doing, we suffer and feel suffocated, so we look for freedom.

When a philosophy is high, an immature student may misunderstand or misapply it. This has happened in the East—the philosophy was very profound, but the masses were not ready for it. When some people heard the concept of not being the doer but simply being a seer, they started believing too much in determinism and became more fatalistic—since everything is determined, why care? The purpose of this philosophy was to liberate the mind from body-consciousness, but ordinary people were not ready for it and they took it literally. Instead of putting effort into being active, they became lazy and inactive. People of the East believe in fate, not in an enlightened way but in a negative way, "If I am poor, if I am sick, if I am fat, it's just the way it's supposed to be, so let it be." That's not the right attitude. One has to work very hard to realize the pure light of awareness. It is very subtle work. East can learn from West how to be dynamic and active, while West can learn from East how to be content and serene.

Belief
and
Action

M ANY PEOPLE subscribe to concepts without really
using them to change the quality of their lives. People
often repeat that they believe in God; but what does it
mean? They also believe in Mars and Venus; what's the
difference? If you are cheating and hurting others while
saying, "I believe in God," what does this statement mean?
Ordinary people just adopt such statements without check-
ing into their lives to see how they are living. Unless God
lives through you, unless the memory of God manifests
itself through your actions, unless and until your actions
indicate that when you do something you feel it is God's
energy working through your hands, "I believe in God" is
simply a concept, like "I believe in the moon."

God means cosmic energy. When you meet others, you
see God. You are not dealing with ordinary mortals, you
are dealing with God in so many forms. How can you be
disrespectful? How can you tease or hurt God? When you
bring this awareness of love and trust to your relationships
with others, then you really believe in God. "I believe in
God" is an empty statement unless we live a life of trust,
love, and freedom from worries. If I believe in God, why

should I worry? He, She, or It knows where I should go, and puts me there. God has not given me the advantage of always feeling bliss, but God has put me wherever I can grow best.

The child of wisdom is born when we are ready to bear the labor pain of Divine love confidently, bravely, and graciously. Divine love means sharing, trusting, and keeping our minds free from worries about the future. Why worry whether you will eat or have a bank account tomorrow? Can't you celebrate five minutes of freedom now? Five minutes is a long time—three hundred seconds. Can't you celebrate just one second with joy and freedom? When you put your total energy into celebrating freedom, love, joy, and beauty, you go beyond the dimension of time, beyond the dimension of measuring. That is where grace works. As long as we are concerned with time, with cause and effect, we are living in the same, ordinary dimension of life, with all its problems. Only when we expose ourselves—as in, "Follow me, let the dead bury their dead"—do we grow and shine.

The East does not emphasize martyrdom; the West does. In the West, you always have to be giving, giving, giving and never have fun, as though having fun is falling into disaster and sinfulness. The eastern approach allows you to have fun. You don't have to be a martyr to be enlightened.

Self-Acceptance
and
The Focal Point

IF YOU ACCEPT yourself as you are for only five minutes, you will get a glimpse of joy and freedom. Then that glimpse automatically will pull you, and you won't have to be always convincing yourself intellectually and theoretically. When you first saw Niagara Falls or fell in love or had sex or had your first drink, the power of the falls, the love, or the sex automatically pulled you toward it. You didn't have to request your mind, "Please think of sex, think of alcohol, think of Niagara Falls." There is something inherently wonderful in those things that makes you think of them. In the same way, there is something wonderful in that Divine dimension of freedom, joy, grace, and love. Once you expose yourself and take a chance, your mind is automatically pulled forever in that direction.

What do you do when you don't accept yourself? What do you do when you do accept yourself? When you don't accept the way your body is, you exercise. When you don't accept how your clothes are, you wash them. When you don't accept feeling hungry, you eat; but when you have eaten, do you take time to accept yourself and realize, "Now I feel all right"?

When you cannot accept not being creative and dynamic, you work all day. When you retire and go to sleep, you accept yourself. Even if your bed is not perfect and your partner is ugly, after some time you yawn and fall asleep. The Eastern approach allows us to accept that we may forget each other in the flow of life. We all forget ourselves unconsciously during sleep; so, too, we have to learn to forget ourselves in a conscious way. Only when we learn to forget ourselves by surrendering or watching our emotions, thoughts, and feelings will we realize the Divine beauty of life.

"Thou art That" is the Eastern saying. It means "I am absolute consciousness." Here you find, "Be still and know that I am God," and "Whosoever saves his life will lose it; whosoever loses his life for My sake will save it." Why are you fearful? What are you going to lose? Whatever you are afraid to lose, you will lose anyway. You already have lost beauty and youth, but you are holding onto your shadow. Let go of your shadow. So little time is left. In the little time that is left, you can enjoy life in a very free and easy way.

In all Eastern and Western approaches, the technique that will help you do this is to emphasize a focal point. Different people may require different focal points—perhaps selfless service, or prayer, or a mantra, or meditation. It doesn't matter, because it is not your prayer, meditation, or selfless service that will liberate you; it is your acceptance of yourself. When you meditate, you think, "Now I am good, now I am Divine, now I am behaving myself." When you serve others, you think, "Now I am selfless, I am living the life of a dignified, gentle person." When you pray, you think, "Now I am devotional and submitting to God's will." You accept yourself when you follow your focal point, so the key is self-acceptance.

If you are sick, it is very difficult to accept yourself even if you want to. It is easier to accept yourself when you are healthy. You feel good mental health through a focal point. If you meditate and visualize some Divine form, you appreciate yourself at that moment because mind is centered, and you are doing what you are supposed to be doing. When you appreciate yourself for doing what you are supposed to be doing, you go beyond yourself. When you go beyond yourself, there is a Divine grace, a Divine dimension of love, light, joy, and oneness.

Tonight, I lost my temper with one of the students who was going to drive me to the lecture. I never like to be late, especially when I am to give a talk, and she was fifteen minutes late. I took my bag and threw it to the side to make the point. I thought if I could throw something, she would remember and try harder to be on time. She said, "Swamiji, you know I am helpless."

I said, "I am also helpless to not do what I am doing!"

She asked, "How can I improve myself and accept myself? I hate myself."

I said, "I hate myself too. How can we accept ourselves?"

We all get angry. We all lose our balance. Yet we have to see that it passes, it does not stay with us permanently; and we do not have to feel guilty about it. We can be playful about our moods and see that we don't get stuck with them. We can accept ourselves only as Godself. As long as we identify with our individual consciousness as a person, a woman, or a man, we will never be able to accept ourselves in the real sense. We will think, "I am a little chubby, I am singing off key, my mind is not attuned" and always find something that is not totally acceptable. It is natural to go through ups and downs, so develop a playful, accepting attitude, and through a focal point keep your mind centered and attuned. When you transcend yourself, you find that behind your normal, usual self there is a Divine Self, a

225

cosmic Self. In the beginning, we can only recognize the Godself by first accepting the mere self.

SELFLESS
LOVE

IN ADDITION TO the focal point, all religions emphasize selfless love. You have lived many years and are always busy. Even if you live a thousand years, you will keep busy and never have free time unless you deliberately create a time. The ability to create time indicates how wise or messed up you are. Think how many people you could make happy if you wrote a letter every month. Many people are eager to hear from you. Since you are not reaching them, and they are not reaching you, they are feeling lonely, you are feeling lonely, and there is no flow of Divine love. Through a focal point, you become faithful to yourself. Through selfless love, you go out of your limited body-consciousness. You show faith in the universal consciousness. That is taught in all religions and philosophies. When you are in touch with that space of Divine love, you are no longer identified with being a man or a woman, Eastern or Western. These distinctions all dissolve.

Have a journal, and in it write down the good and bad things you do each day. That awareness will help keep you attuned and direct your time and energy toward useful things.

The West's emphasis on differentiations and divisions

create rifts and pains in our psyche, and lack of acceptance is behind so many psychological problems. In the East, people have been able to accept themselves and their weaknesses. Because they are lazier, they have more poverty there, whereas here we are more dynamic, so there is more affluence.

Our philosophy determines the quality of our life, so set aside five minutes every day to accept yourself the way you are. That is your meditation. Sit down in an easy chair and don't watch television. Even if you feel bored, don't run away from boredom. Accept the boredom. After some time, you will find that you are feeling good, and you are in touch with that Divine space which is beyond Eastern and Western boundaries.

ACTION
AND
REACTION

THE PHILOSOPHY of karma is interesting but not well understood. It suggests that you are the author of your destiny, you are responsible for what you are, and you have the power to be what you decide to be. The whole responsibility falls on your shoulders. Through this philosophy you are exposed to a dimension of being that has so much power, potential, and zeal that you can accept and face the responsibilities and challenges of life without any hesitation.

You can accept the responsibilities and challenges of life in the same way that you accept the hairs on your head.

You spend a few minutes every day washing and combing your hair, and you enjoy that. When you start losing your hair, you know that your responsibility is becoming less, but you don't enjoy that because it is more fun to have lots of hair. As you don't feel burdened by hairs, so you should not feel burdened by the challenges and responsibilities of life. What would life be if you did not have them? Would you rather be a rock, having no sensitivity, no responsibilities, no feelings? Or would you rather be a human being with ups and downs, who knows that no matter how many times you go through those ups and downs you maintain your Divine changelessness?

REAPING
AS
YOU SOW

WHEN WE USE the word karma, we mean action—but action that necessarily has a reaction. There is no action without reaction. You reap as you sow. If you are going to reap as you sow, you should be careful what you sow. You sow the seeds of your destiny through the way you think, the way you plan, the way you fantasize, the way you deal with fellow beings.

Many of us like to blame our parents, society, or religion for what we are because we are not yet in touch with our own compulsiveness, laziness, indecisiveness, and fearfulness. But ever since you got in touch with yourself and felt that you could take care of yourself, you accepted the challenge of becoming what you wanted to be. Have you been faithful to that? Have you always followed your conscience? When a lotus blossoms, does it criticize the mud where it got its birth? You are what you are, not because of this society, good or bad, but because of what you deserved to be. Do you have a loving heart for yourself and your fellow beings? Do you feel the need to cultivate that love? If you feel that sweet urge in your heart to cultivate love and compassion, for what can you blame society? Through

231

the philosophy of karma we become very careful, very thoughtful about our deeds and thoughts.

CATEGORIES
OF
KARMA

KARMA IS DIVIDED into three categories. The first is called *prarabdha* karma—active impressions. This refers to those impressions, seeds, or actions of past lives that are bearing fruit in this lifetime. The body you have, the parents you have, the material situations you have been in are the result of prarabdha karma. Prarabdha karma is karma that has started bearing fruit.

The second category is *sanchit* karma—stored impressions, those seeds that are waiting for germination. In your past lives, you were doing different things, cultivating different tendencies, different desires. All those impressions are stored in your psyche. The third category is called *kriyamana* karma—that karma which we are now expressing. I am creating seeds for future impressions by the way I talk, the way I relate to you, the way I react to the way you relate to me.

There is a subtle difference between kriyamana karma and prarabdha karma. It is because of our prarabdha karma that we are meeting right now. Prarabdha karma provides us with a particular setting and situation. That setting or situation does not determine our actions, thoughts, desires and emotions. Once we are together, however, it is kriyamana karma that determines how we relate and respond to each other.

Most of us think, "It is just my karma." It may be your karma that you are born into a poor or rich family, but prarabdha karma never determines that you will steal because you are poor. If you are poor, you can work hard to earn an honest living. The way you live your life in spite of being rich or poor is the result of kriyamana karma. In kriyamana karma, you are free to act.

Through free will, you use your intelligence and power of discrimination. You can choose what makes you loving, secure, and fearless, and avoid those thoughts and actions that make you insecure, selfish, unloving, unforgiving, and fearful. It is through your own understanding and free will in any given time and situation that your prarabdha karma leads you into good or bad actions and the resulting feelings of contentment or remorse. When you use your power of choice properly, you feel good about yourself. You rejoice in your Divine Essence. In spite of all your spiritual training and understanding and no matter how many people love and respect you, if you misuse your power of choice, you feel bad about yourself.

You can test whether or not this philosophy of karma applies in your life. If you did not feel guilty or proud of your actions, you would be completely free of the wheel of karma; but as long as you feel insecure, guilty, or proud, you are under the influence of karma. As long as you feel guilty or proud, you are accepting responsibility for your actions as a doer and acknowledging that you have the choice of doing right or wrong.

ॐ

KARMA
AND
DESTINY

MANY OF US like to dump everything on prarabdha karma or destiny, but as long as you feel guilty or proud or blame others—"This person was dishonest, this person cheated me, hurt me or robbed me"—you cannot say that everything is happening just because of destiny. If it is happening because of destiny, how can you feel hurt and blame others? It was destined to happen.

The concept of destiny is misleading. If you can totally believe that whatever happens to you and to others is because of destiny, then who will blame whom, and who will praise whom? As long as there is guilt or pride, praise or blame, it is not all destiny, and you have to acknowledge your capacity to choose your own course of action. You also have a choice of motives, so how can you say it is happening by destiny?

Suppose you did your best but could not make as much money as others, or be as successful as others. You have to accept that this is because of past karma: others are better equipped to be talented musicians, painters, speakers, or doctors. This concept gives comfort. You are whatever you are because of past impressions.

KARMA
AND
SELF-ACCEPTANCE

THROUGH understanding prarabdha karma, we develop a sense of self-acceptance. Once you accept yourself the way you are and at the same time accept responsibility to choose your present course of actions with understanding, wisdom, and conscience, then you go beyond the realm of choosing, beyond the realm of free will—and even beyond the realm of karma. Use your free will judiciously. Then you find that your free will is just an expression of Divine Will.

As long as you are not quite integrated, not quite evolved, you will have a sense of responsibility about what is right and what is wrong and feel proud or guilty. Once your life is integrated in the light of your own conscience, understanding, and wisdom, then you realize, "It was just Divine Will, and I thought it was my will." When you realize this higher dimension of will, you are free from self-pity and fear.

Self-pity deprives us of the beauty of the past; fear deprives us of the beauty of the future; and jealousy deprives us of the beauty of the moment. Otherwise, isn't life beautiful? When we look at life through those screens of self-pity, jealousy, and fear, the world appears distorted. When the screens are no longer there and we are able to relate to life and to the world with the light of love and acceptance, we are filled with beauty, joy, and peace.

This example illustrates the difference among the three karmas: Suppose you go to a library and take out a few books. The book that you start to study is your prarabdha karma. The notes you prepare from that book and your plans to get other books based on those notes are your kriyamana karma; and all the books that you will read later come under the category of sanchit karma.

The enlightened person who has real wisdom stops preparing notes. He has no need for notes and no desire to consult any more books. He knows the Truth, and that's it. He continues to read and enjoy the book that he has taken from the library and started to read. He is stuck with that book, but he will never consult other books that are on the shelf; his own body is his book. If you reach enlightenment, you will never bother to fulfill all the karmas, all the impressions and unmanifest desires in your psyche, because you already feel full within yourself.

Prarabdha karma is that karma which has brought you to this body and situation; it is the result of your past actions.

Kriyamana karma is that karma with which you act, react, and plan at the moment.

Sanchit karmas are those past impressions that have not yet started manifesting their fruits. For example, suppose that there are many lawsuits against you at a particular time. One case is being heard in the court; others are waiting to be heard later. Sanchit karmas are those cases that are waiting to be heard. Once you are enlightened, they are never heard; they are just burnt.

INCLINATIONS
AND
TENDENCIES

THE PHILOSOPHY of karma gives us the understanding that we all have different tendencies and inclinations. If you observe two or three children of the same parents, you find that even though each of them has been raised in the same setting, one wants to be a singer, another wants to be a painter, and another wants to be a monk. They were exposed to the same life, yet they have different inclinations.

Unless we trace back beyond our parents to our past lives, we cannot explain the diversity of nature that we find in one another. If only our parents or a particular social setting were responsible for our being what we are, then children of the same parents raised and trained in the same society would have similar inclinations; but that is not the case. Through this philosophy of karma, we have a better understanding of how we have different inclinations and skills. You may want to become a great singer but not be able to become a great singer; you may want to be a great spiritual person but not be able to control your senses and direct your mind to higher dimensions. What happens to those good intentions when you die?

Your Efforts
Are Never
Wasted

ALTHOUGH YOU may not reach your destination, this philosophy of karma assures you that your efforts are never wasted. In the Divine scheme, whatever effort you put in any direction is taken into account—an ethereal or akashic account, you might say. According to that account, you will be blessed with another birth, and in that birth you will follow the same pattern and not have to start from A. If you have gone from A to B, then you start at B to reach Z. If you have gone up to C or H, then you start from there. If you don't believe in the philosophy of karma, then it becomes almost impossible to understand your failures and successes on different levels. The philosophy of karma gives a helpful explanation. To be held up in heaven or hell does not give you a process of gradual growth. Through this philosophy of karma, you can understand that to whatever extent you make progress here, you will start from there in your next life; and that goes on and on until you reach final liberation. In final liberation, you are freed of all karmas.

Those people who are enlightened and have reached the ultimate state of consciousness say that enlightenment is possible in this life. Although they were enlightened, their bodies acted through the effect of prarabdha karma. Prarabdha karma is that karma which produces the body, so whatever is already there for the body to go through, such as a sickness, an accident, a big event, certain insults or injuries, has to be gone through. But if the soul within the body is enlightened, it remains detached and does not over-react. You take things casually, as though watching a movie. If the movie is great, you laugh or cry; if the movie is lousy, you just dismiss it. But whether you laugh or cry, you don't keep brooding about the movie. You know it was just a movie. When an enlightened person goes through ups and downs, he takes those events as parts of the setting of a movie. He is always free, always detached, always established in his Essence; but as long as he is living, he has to go through his karma.

If you read the lives of great mystics in different religions, you find that some became sick; some became rich; some were scholarly; some were like dumb persons, not caring about the world and remaining aloof; and some behaved as if they were mad. You find different types of behavior in enlightened persons. There is not one particular way for enlightened beings to behave. Their bodies go through highs and lows in different ways. This is all the effect of prarabdha karma.

An enlightened sage was walking along when he saw a man beating another man. He stopped and asked, "Why are you beating him? What is wrong?"

The man who was doing the beating shouted, "This man has borrowed money from me and not returned it. How dare you interfere? Shut up!" And he pushed the enlightened man, who fell unconscious to the ground.

When the disciples of the sage heard that their teacher was hurt, they rushed to him and started fanning him. After a while, the old man became conscious. The disciples wanted to be sure he was all right, so they asked him, "Who is fanning you?"

The teacher replied, "The one who pushed me is now fanning me."

He made no distinction between the one who hurt him and the one who fanned him. The differentiating reasoning leaves the mind of those who are enlightened or very advanced on the spiritual ladder. Until we are that advanced, we have to use our free will and discrimination in whatever situation we are in.

———————————

KARMA
AND
SOUL-SATISFACTION

How will you use this free will to be free of the cycle of karma? One way is to keep in touch with yourself, and to know what gives you soul-satisfaction versus what is just surface satisfaction. If you were given a choice to repeat seven days or seven events of your life, which would you like to repeat again and again? You would pick those days and experiences in which you were closest to yourself.

Many times I have very easy days: I get good food, I get plenty of sleep, I see beautiful flowers, birds, and faces; but if I were asked later if I would like to repeat those days, I would say no because I was not in attunement. Although it was pleasant, it did not give me that soul-satisfaction. It was fun but only on the surface.

I seldom find any thought worth thinking; yet mind keeps busily thinking. This is nonsense, is it not? It is the same with talking. We are so insecure about each other or ourselves that we fill up the space between us with words to avoid each other. We don't want anyone to enter into our private space, so we defend ourselves with a wall of words behind which we think others will not know us directly. It is really soothing when people don't have to talk but can just enjoy each other's company.

Do those things that bring you back to yourself, things that keep you in touch with yourself. "In touch with yourself" means in touch with your awareness, in touch with your Divine Essence. But such mystical terms aren't really necessary. You don't have to believe in God to be spiritual, and you don't have to believe in God to be healthy and peaceful. There have been great seers who realized that supreme peace without believing in God. Buddha was one of them. If God makes no sense to you, don't believe in God; but believe in yourself. You have to believe in yourself even to deny yourself. Try to deny yourself without believing in yourself. Who will deny? You have to be there to deny yourself. You know you cannot deny yourself, so the question is how can you keep in touch with yourself?

You Are
the
Knower

MANY PEOPLE say they cannot concentrate. Don't worry about concentrating the mind. If you can see that the mind is restless, that is more than concentration. When you are able to see that your mind is restless, keep watching the restlessness of the mind. Remember, you are the knower of the restlessness of the mind. The more you develop this awareness that you are the watcher, the knower of the restlessness of the mind, the more you develop peace, attunement and joy. The more you identify with the restless mind, the more you cannot know that your mind is restless because you become the mind. If you know your mind is restless, you know you are not the mind; you are someone who knows the mind. So keep noticing.

The more you notice the restlessness of the mind, the more you notice the stability of yourself. We appreciate light because we know darkness. We know good health because we have known sickness. We know love because we are familiar with fear and hatred. How can you appreciate the stable, changeless nature of your being without noticing, in contrast, the restlessness of the mind? To get in touch with that changeless nature of your being, develop the habit of noticing the changing nature of your mind.

The highest moments of my life were those of pure awareness. I am still not capable of tuning into those blissful moments all the time, so I compromise with thoughts or a movie or anything that comes along. You have to make compromises, but you have to know you cannot get permanent satisfaction from these compromises. Permanent satisfaction will come only when your mind is able to tune into its Source, that awareness which is filled with bliss. As long as mind is not capable of tuning into that Source, you have to make compromises. So accept your humanness.

There is nothing wrong in craving beauty, money, youthfulness, power, fame, or anything else—but these are not going to give soul-satisfaction, because they take the mind away from its Source. If you find happiness in things, you will remain dependent and fearful because your happiness is at the mercy of something other than yourself. But when you know that you are Divine, that you are one with the cosmos, even if you don't feel that high all the time, you have that knowledge and it gives you a sense of eternal freedom.

It's Smart
To Be Dumb

THROUGH YOU, I remember my own student life. In those days I went through a lot of upheavals, and what comforted me at that time was hearing, "To be great is to be misunderstood." The more I was misunderstood by my friends, relatives, and teachers, the more I thought I was going to be great. So I hope some of you can carry that conviction within you when you are misunderstood by your peers and so-called scholarly teachers.

I was not a dumb student, but I think the greatest lesson one can learn in life is to be dumb. One is wise when one can accept and be at ease about one's foolishness. Even the topic for this lecture is dumb—squeezing the Spirit into the student's body. It should be the other way—squeezing the student's body into the Spirit. The body does not have to be squeezed into the Spirit. Aeroplanes fly freely in space, and since Spirit is bigger than space, all bodies can fly in this Spirit.

Why do you really care for smartness? I have not found that those who are settled and have become doctors, professors, scientists, and so-called geniuses to be particularly smart. They are as dumb as any one of us. They have a special merit in a particular field. We can value and appreciate that and learn something from them; but when it comes to life, they are as insecure, compulsive, undisciplined, scattered, and selfish as anyone else. If they are not selfish and insecure, it is not because they were taught not to be in college.

Our emphasis is totally wrong. I don't know what people mean when they speak in terms of "intelligence" and "wisdom." Through intelligence you will know many things about life, the world, and relationships—but what about knowing knowing? You know me. You notice my presence because of your eyesight. If I were not here and someone else were sitting on the chair, would you not notice him? Are you seeing because of me, or is your eyesight independent of the one who takes this chair? You are listening to me, but if someone else were speaking, you would still be listening. Your hearing is not dependent on what you hear or on the speaker.

This applies to all your senses, and it applies to your knowing. You have this power of knowing, power of awareness, power of consciousness. Through this power of knowing you know your thoughts, emotions, feelings, fantasies, fears, and guilts. You may not know what I know, and I may not know what you know, but we all know that we know.

We put too much energy into what we know or could know to influence others by our smartness. What about pure knowing, pure awareness? Pure knowing cannot be known in a dualistic sense. When I know you, you are separate from me; when you know me, I am separate from you. There is a duality. Any object that is known is separate from the knower. But when it comes to knowing, itself, there is no longer a subject-object relationship. That's why it becomes mystical, transcendental, universal, and liberating. That's why it gives you the power of love, selflessness, and humility. You know it is the same knowing here, there, and everywhere.

Nobody is smarter and nobody is dumber; it only appears so on the surface.

———————————

—From a lecture at Macalester College, Minneapolis, 1989

KNOW
KNOWING

WHAT DO YOU want to know, and why do you want to know? No matter what you know, it can never help you to know knowing. You may not know physics, chemistry, singing, or dancing, but as long as you know that you know it doesn't matter what you know or don't know. Even if you don't know my name, at least you know that you don't know it. You cannot deny your knowing. You have an awareness of knowing, and through that knowing you either know something or don't know something. That knowing is independent of knowing or not knowing that particular thing. Knowing is universal. All intellectual and material knowledge is limited. All the mystics, all the evolved souls, were highly advanced not because they knew more than you and I but because they were in touch with this universal, pure knowing. They had access to that pure awareness that is shining in you and in me.

Get in touch with your knowing. When you are not awake in the morning, the sun is still shining. In winter when you don't go to the ocean, ocean is still there. Your real knowing remains unaffected by your intellectual knowing. You may not understand something, but you understand that you don't understand. Pure knowing is always there and has nothing to do with what you understand or don't understand. Don't delude yourself that when you finally understand all the mystical teachings, you will be in touch with knowing. Your knowing is free of all these things. It exists here and now.

How can we get in touch with this knowing? By conserving our energy from knowing objects. If I allow my energy to become exhausted in the process of knowing what I want to know, then what is left over for knowing knowing itself? See this point very clearly. Nothing else will be this important in your life, whether you become a doctor or a typist. If you know this knowing, you are much better than any doctor who doesn't know this knowing. It is very abstract. Let us take some help from our day-to-day experiences. Off and on, you catch yourself daydreaming and find yourself lost in your fantasies and fears, guilts and insecurities. How did you catch yourself to notice that you were lost in brooding and daydreaming? What is the difference between the two experiences, being lost and being suddenly awake and alert?

When you catch yourself daydreaming and are back to yourself, what do you know about yourself at that moment? When you see that you were lost in something other than yourself, what do you know about yourself at the moment of clarity? You know something, but you will not be able to put it into words. Similarly, if I meet you after a year and don't recognize you, and you tell me that you are the person whom I saw at this college, I might ask you, "How do you know you are the same person?" You just know you are the same self. Wherein lies this sameness? Does it lie in your nose, in your eyes, in your lips, in your looks, in your relationships? Whether you are successful or unsuccessful, beautiful or ugly, intelligent or dumb, this current of sameness stays intact within you.

We are talking about this essence of sameness in a theoretical way, but how do we get the feel of it in a realistic sense? Take a comfortable position. Close your eyes and take a few deep breaths ... Then let your breathing be normal, keep your eyes closed, and watch the process of breathing through your nostrils ... Now, while you are breathing, start counting ... When you breathe in, count one; when you breathe out, count two; breathe in, three; breathe out, four. Count like that up to twenty and then reverse the process of counting: breathe in twenty, breathe out nineteen ... Do it very carefully until you come to zero, and when you reach zero, get in touch with what is there and how you are in touch with that. When you are finished, rub your palms and put them around your face ...

Did you feel a sense of wholeness, a sense of contentment, a sense of more ease and acceptance? You know nothing, yet you miss nothing. You don't care to know anything because you have a sense of contentment, a sense of satisfaction. The experience of fullness that you have in the unconsciousness of sleep can be had consciously when you become aware of awareness itself. When you have a certain thought, desire, or fear, you have to attend to it; when you work on a computer, you have to use your mind. But when you are not required to keep thinking, you can watch your thoughts and feelings as a witness. The thought or feeling is a stranger passing by the door of your consciousness. You are not to interact but simply notice it and let it go.

When you let a thought or fantasy go, you are back to yourself. Only because you get involved with the thought or fantasy do you not get to know yourself as you are. If you are involved with something other than yourself, how can you know yourself? You have become so addicted to flirting with these thoughts that it is very difficult not to get carried away with them. As you practice self-awareness, you will find that thoughts are separate from awareness. Think, brood, or fantasize as much as you want. When you are finished thinking, bring your mind back to awareness.

You have a home. You may go out to a movie, to a park, to a feast, or to a date, but you come back to your home. Most of you like to get back to your home. Maybe a few would like to run away. So run away, and take your girl-friend or boyfriend with you. But you have to live some-where, and that becomes your home. Even if you are kidnapped, you settle down somewhere, and wherever you settle down becomes your home. When you go out again, you come back to your home. Where is the home for your mind? Let your mind run away with some fantasy, some sweetheart, but let it settle down somewhere, let it find a home.

It does not have to be mystical. Those who are mixed up want others to remain mixed up so they can have a sense of security about themselves that they are not the only ones who are mixed up. You can have any simple thing as a focal point, a resting place, a home for your awareness. Attend to everything, but don't forget to come back. We come back anyway, even if we are lost. Even if we drink, even if we take drugs, somehow, somewhere we realize what is happening and where we are. There is a cosmic scheme going on that does not permit us to remain lost forever. But those of us who are more intelligent and dedicated follow certain guidelines that help keep us awake and free.

—From a lecture at Macalester College, Minneapolis, 1989

FEARLESSNESS

W ITH THIS understanding, develop a sense of fearlessness. It is at this stage of life that you can learn to be either sissy or fearless. I know many of you are quite fearless in drinking and taking drugs and fooling around, but is that really fearlessness? Does being like a dog peeing anywhere indicate fearlessness? Fearlessness means you know your convictions and stand for those convictions. When you act like an instinctive animal doing things compulsively here and there, it does not indicate that you are fearless. It is at this stage of life, my friends, that you can take chances and be fearless. The more you are fearless, the more life is fun for you.

In your communications, in your writings, in your actions, exude that fearlessness. Ask yourself, "What am I going to lose? People will think that if I make a mistake, I am dumb, and I already know I am dumb." The real learning starts with the recognition of dumbness. That dumbness belongs to the mind. Sometimes mind is dull, sometimes mind is smart. Sometimes body looks healthy, sometimes body looks sickly. Am I this body and mind, or am I that Essence of life that reveals the different states of body and mind? If I were simply a thought, then when that thought is gone, I should be gone. If I were simply a feeling, then when the feeling is gone, I should be gone. If my existence depended on a relationship, then when the relationship is gone, I should be gone. I was born a cute baby, but I am no longer a cute baby; yet I cannot say that because my babyhood is gone, I am gone. I am still here. Something within me remains intact in spite of all the changes that my body and mind go through.

Allow yourself to look dumb, and that is how you learn to be courageous and fearless. As long as you are on guard that you should not look dumb, you are really dumb. When you don't care if you look dumb, you are really smart. We love children because they are so spontaneous; they are not self-consciousness. The more education we get, the more showy and self-conscious we become: "Is my makeup right, do I look smart?"

Be yourself.

Do you want to get high? You might have tried some intoxicants, but how long do you want to continue that pattern? If you want to continue, okay, but is life meant only for those goofy things? How can you be happy about yourself? Just having a pleasurable experience is never going to make you happy, because you are not just an ordinary animal. You have wisdom in you that will make you feel rotten about yourself. You cannot run away from self-remorse. Thank God that you feel guilty and remorseful. It is only through this healthy guilt and remorse that you are going to change your negative patterns.

As long as you are undisciplined, you can never have self-esteem and freedom. When you have a sense of self-mastery, you enjoy life's simple pleasures much more deeply; but when you indulge in those pleasures compulsively, you are just a victim of your negative habits and are bound to resent being a victim. Shake off those negative habits—the sooner the better.

Don't think that because others are goofing off you also should goof off. Once I was in a hospital where many people were suffering and dying. It never struck me that since those others were suffering and dying, I should also suffer and die. Who wants to live in that horrible hospital? Even if the whole world is suffering and dying, a few of us must get out of that sick hospital and try to help those who are stuck there.

You want to love and help others. You want to share money or gifts or give a massage to make others happy. But if you are not doing any of these things but can simply look dumb, you serve others because when they see how dumb you are, they feel a little smarter and better about themselves.

Once there was a cat. Many mice lived where the cat was living. One day, the family of mice was having a big conference to decide how to deal with this cat. They decided to tie a bell around the cat's neck so they would know in advance when she was coming. The question was, who would tie the bell around the cat's neck? They were all holding back like you and me, feigning holiness. But holiness comes from fire; holiness challenges fire.

My friends, it is time for you to really decide whether you are going to be like Lincoln, Martin Luther King, Gandhi, Kennedy, or Mother Teresa. Be fearless. Have a clear goal. I don't find students here reading biographies and autobiographies of these great men and women. I heartily recommend that you read the lives of great people. Even if you want to remain lethargic, dumb, and lost, there is a great power in those books that will shake up your laziness, fear, and insecurity, and inspire you to manifest your Divine strength. You have too low an image of yourself. You want to be a doctor, an engineer, an attorney. That's nonsense. Be a man of courage and compassion. Be a woman of love and light.

Be a little meditative. Don't think that meditation has anything to do with religion. As you take a shower without thinking that the shower will make you religious, why can't you meditate, why can't you calm down, why can't you talk with the flowers and birds? You are goofing off anyway— why not learn to goof off in the name of meditation? Have a good time. Sometimes you feel guilty about not being productive. Relax! Do you want to produce more nuclear bombs so we can kill each other faster? It is great to hold back a little; relax and be filled with loving energy, zeal, confidence, and fearlessness, and be of service to others. There is no higher joy in life than making others joyful.

———————————

—From a lecture at Macalester College, Minneapolis, 1989

SHARING
WITH A DOG

O NE DAY WHILE I was living in a cave, a dog followed me. For supper, I had only three small *puris,* which are fried breads. I am a bit of a miser, a little on the selfish side, so that evening was a test for me. Here was a dog, and I had only three small breads. I was hungry, and they were not enough even for me. I wondered, "Should I eat them myself or give some to the dog?" After a lot of internal discussion, I felt maybe I could give half of one bread to the dog. After a while, I gave him another half too. I started eating and realized I was eating two, so I thought it would be more fair if I gave one and a half to the dog and ate one and a half myself. As I was eating, I thought that it was just what an ordinary person would do, and since I was living in the cave to be something more than just ordinary, I decided to give two to the dog and one to myself. Later on, that dog became one of my closest friends, and even today I remember that sharing with the utmost joy and satisfaction. I have shared many things in my life, but that was one of the most profound sharings. It healed my heart and opened something within me.

Don't think that one day when you have so much

money, so much time, so much something, that then you will share. You can share now. You can write a simple note to someone: "Mom, I love you." "Dear friend, I miss you, you have inspired me in many ways." Take time to write; take time to fix a cup of tea for your friends; take time to give a massage to someone who needs one. Don't think it is not a "great" act. The way we measure greatness is indicative of our ego. Any simple act is very, very great if you do it with love and oneness. Spare a dime or a dollar to be of service to someone. It will enhance your self-esteem, and you will feel good about yourself. The greatest art of life is to feel happy by making someone else happy and thereby realize the mystical thread of life.

Be fearless, be disciplined, be meditative, and be selfless. That will make you happy and playful. Do some exercise to keep your body healthy, and don't always rush. Have five or ten minutes for meditation. If you can learn one simple thing in your entire life, you will have learned all things, because all things are hidden in every thing. If you transcend your ego, you have learned everything. Then the student's body will be filled with Divine Spirit.

—From a lecture at Macalester College, Minneapolis, 1989

FEELING
WORTHY

COUNTLESS BLOCKS get in the way of enlightenment, but the greatest is a sense of worthlessness. You feel, "There may be God, there may be enlightenment, there may be grace, but I don't deserve it."

When you sincerely and honestly work for a long time to remove your blocks, you develop a sense of self-worth. You feel as if you deserve the enlightenment you seek. When you believe that you deserve it, you are blessed with it. This is the real meaning of the word "faith." When you have that faith, you know that whether you are good or bad, God is supporting you, has been supporting you, and will continue to support you. This sense of self-worth is the most important aspect of faith. Self-worth means, "I deserve it." It's not that you demand it; it's just that you deserve it.

When you wake up in the morning and the sun is shining, you enjoy the sunshine. On a warm day, you open your doors and windows to enjoy the sunshine even more. Knowing that you deserve it allows you to enjoy it. You don't command the sun to rise for you—you trust, and it rises anyway.

You take ordinary, mundane things for granted. When you come home from your job (even if your boss has annoyed you), you do certain rituals to make the transition from work to home. Perhaps you turn on the television. If so, you trust that it will work. You embrace your husband or wife, hug your child, pat your dog. You take them for granted. If you don't have these creatures to embrace, you embrace your whiskey bottle, trusting that *it* is going to work. See how much trust you have even in a bottle of whiskey? You feel safe in that trust.

The Life Force causes the sun to rise. It is more reliable than anything you can imagine—sun, moon, ocean, earth—but somehow you don't trust it. Yet Divine Providence has always supported you and will always support you, even if you don't trust it. The faith you have in your whiskey, girlfriend, boyfriend, or television—have that simple faith in divine light, love, and grace. Then you will definitely have it. All spiritual disciplines are meant to develop this trust, this faith in divine grace. So what should you do, become, or achieve to have this trust that lets you know that you deserve?

DESERVING
GOD'S
GRACE

As LONG AS YOU do not have a mental problem, you know that you are you: you are Ray, Shantanand, Marvin, Ruth, or whoever. But who is this "Ray," who is this "Shantanand"? If I meet you ten years from now and cannot recognize you, you will remind me that we met ten years before. If I ask you, "How do you know you are the same person?", you may wonder if I have gone crazy.

In the core of your being and in the core of my being, we know we continue to be the same. Many things about me change—my body, my looks, my thoughts, my relationships, my imaginations and fantasies, my values and standards—but something within me remains the same and transcends all these changes. Can you sense this changeless essence in yourself? You may not be able to objectify it and see it, but do you sense something in you that is changeless?

If, in spite of all the changes on the periphery of your being, you are the same, then what are you striving to do to make you what you are not? Do you want to become something you are not? Or do you want to know what you really are? Where should you go, what should you look for, what should you accomplish to know yourself as you really are?

Enlightenment is the realization of the essence of your being which supports your personality, struggles, and experiences. Like water in a lake, there may be waves, ripples, or bubbles, but behind all these is water. This essence is in all our experiences, negative or positive. That's how you know you are the same, despite surface changes. The path of *devotion* brings you to a place where you can trust that you deserve divine grace and are worthy of realizing it everywhere. If God is mercy and grace, then God must be related to you here and now even in your supposed undeservingness.

No matter how much you struggle or how virtuous you become, unless you develop a sense that you *deserve* God's grace, you will always feel negative and insecure. No matter how wonderful your relationship with electricity and candles, you still need the sun to shine, or there will be too much darkness in the world. So let God's light shine through your "undeservingness," through your anxiety, your fears. Open the doors that you think are closed even to God's grace.

You are used to thinking in terms of what you should do. If you are told to repeat a mantra or get up at five o'clock in the morning and meditate two hours every day, that makes sense to you. If you are told to be selfless, kind, and charitable, that makes sense to you. Yet if you are told to be yourself and open all the doors of your heart to let in the divine breeze, that makes no sense to you. As long as you believe in your ego and doership, you think in terms of doing; you think you can do something to create God's grace and enlightenment.

But the most important thing is just to be yourself. This may include being jealous, insecure, fragmented, and fearful. Accept it. Don't deny it or suppress it. Own it and see how long this negative feeling of fear, jealousy, or insecurity stays in the space of your heart, in the space of your consciousness. Have patience. Don't react. Don't start doing anything. Just be watchful. It may be difficult for you to be watchful; it may be easier to start jogging. If you feel like jogging, jog. If you feel like dancing, dance. Do anything, but be yourself.

If you want to get in touch with the skin of your body, you have to take off your clothes. If you want to take a shower, you have to take off your clothes. You are made of Divine Essence; you are pure Divine Essence; but as long as you stay away from yourself and avoid facing yourself, you cannot get in touch with this Divine Essence. Instead of taking off your clothes, you are putting on more and more. Then you complain you feel itchy.

CREATE A SPACE
FOR PEACE

YOU HAVE TO make a living; you have to cater to your boyfriend, girlfriend, husband, children, cats and dogs; you have to mow the lawn. Enjoy all this busy-ness for a while. God is not in a hurry. God can afford to be without you for some more time. But can you afford to be without God? You need to create a space for God's grace. If I am the one with a closed fist, can I complain that you are not giving me a sweet? Even if you want to, my fist is closed. I'm the one who has to open it.

The mind is constantly complaining, "Without grace there is no peace; I want enlightenment and peace."

God whispers, "Create a space for me, and I will be right there."

"Sorry, sorry," you reply. "I know You are there, and You mean well, but I am busy."

Yet in spite of being busy, every day you spare time to eat, go to the bathroom, sleep, make love. Can't you make some free time now and then for God's grace?

"Flirting" Away
from
Grace

G OD'S GRACE, or enlightenment, is like a prince or princess whom you want to marry. If you are constantly fooling around with other girls and boys, will that divine prince or princess want to marry you? Will hundreds of lovers knocking at your door every minute really make you happy? If you have hundreds of lovers, can you be fully present with any of them? In the same way, you have hundreds of thoughts, fantasies, and interests that you fight with and complain about; yet you are unwilling to release them. Then you say, "There is no grace in my life; how can I find peace?" If you want peace, it is there. Your task is to stop all this flirting.

There are certain needs you cannot avoid. You have to eat, you have to sleep, you have to make a living. So do those things. Then create a space just for peace. Even if peace doesn't come then and there, have patience. Wait. Why are you rushing? Light and joy are coming. When you were a child, could you become an adult in only a few days just because you were impatient? How many years did it take you to become an adult? Peace will come with patience. Create a space and wait. When you create that space, don't watch television, don't call anyone. Just be by yourself for half an hour, and get in touch with your inner peace, poise, inner love, and light and enjoy your restful-ness.

MAKING OTHERS
HAPPY

IF YOU CANNOT handle being by yourself, then you can use a mantra or prayer as your focal point. If you cannot focus on your mantra, then read some holy book or play a tape you like. If you still cannot feel happy, think what you can do selflessly for someone else. If you still don't know what to do, call someone and say you really care, you really love and miss that person.

Human beings need to be loved and needed by others. So take time to make someone feel needed. You may crave hearing that you are important in someone else's life, yet forget that that person might like to hear the same from you. Take time to make someone realize how important he or she has been in your life. Instead of borrowing others' feelings (as in commercial Christmas cards), take time to write something about your own feelings, in your own handwriting. When you borrow feelings, how can you really touch another?

Unless you can make someone happy through some simple act, how can you feel good about yourself? To always receive and never give does not feel good. You have to take the attitude of giver in order to have a positive image about yourself; if you don't have a positive self-image, your mind will brood constantly on your negative patterns.

When you develop a positive image about yourself based on your selflessness, your mind will merge into that pure light in which there is no jealousy, no insecurity, no competition, no struggle.

REGULATING
YOUR LIFE

AFTER CREATING a space for peace, the next step is to lead a regulated life.

If you're currently leading a disordered, unregulated life, don't be too hard on yourself. The first step is to accept your life as it is, accept yourself as you are, and avoid extremes. From there, you can make the desired changes.

The regulation can be done in three phases:

1. Regulate yourself as you are.
2. Incorporate something new that is not too hard.
3. Incorporate the ideal you want to practice in your life, which may be hard.

Regulate Yourself
As You Are

SUPPOSE, for example, that sometimes you wake up at eight o'clock 'n the morning, sometimes at eight-thirty, and sometimes at nine. You don't have to try to get up at six in order to regulate your life. Accept that you get up at eight-thirty or nine; just try to maintain the same time every day. You still can allow yourself ten minutes on a regular basis for inner restfulness and divine attunement.

If your goal, during this first stage of regulation, is to regulate your drinking, don't tell yourself, "I'm going to stop." To develop trust in yourself, do whatever you have been doing—but do it consciously and self-acceptingly. Instead, tell yourself, "I will maintain the same amount of drinking," but regulate it just to the extent that you don't overdo it.

Now, this is very difficult, but it is the first phase of self-regulation. Decide, for example, how much beer is acceptable to you, and tell yourself, "I will drink only this much beer at this time." If you smoke, decide how many cigarettes are acceptable, and tell yourself, "I will smoke only this many cigarettes at these times."

INCORPORATE
SOMETHING NEW
AND NOT TOO HARD

AFTER TWO MONTHS of the first phase, you can start the second phase of self-regulation. Don't rush. Have very simple standards that you think you can easily accomplish. If you have been waking up at eight a.m. for two months, now start waking up at seven-thirty. If you feel you are smoking more than you would like, cut down gradually—maybe by two cigarettes a day.

INCORPORATE
YOUR IDEAL

WHEN YOU HAVE worked with the second phase for two months, move on to the third phase: the way of your ideal. "This is the ideal way I would like to live. I don't want to drink, so I will not drink. I want to get up at five, so I will get up at five." Don't try to incorporate all your ideals at once. That will only create a rift in your psyche. You will think, "I am hopeless because I am not able to do it, and I'll never be able to do it." Even if you are only in the first phase of self-regulation, you can still realize your Divine Essence. Enlightenment does not depend on any regulation (although regulation will help you).

SEE HOW GOD
IS IN YOU
RIGHT NOW

KEEP ACCEPTING yourself throughout the self-regulation process. Say that you retire in a beautiful bedroom, on a beautiful bed, listening to beautiful music and lying down next to a beautiful partner. After some time, you fall asleep and snore. But if you don't have a beautiful bedroom, a beautiful bed, beautiful music, and a beautiful partner to sleep with, what do you do? You fall asleep anyway. That's how much power of endurance and acceptance God has given you. Instead of faulting yourself for not already being where you're trying to get to, ask yourself, "How am I right now?" You don't need to struggle with yourself or aspire to be anything that you are not. You think, "One day I will be holy, I will be regulated, I will be kind and generous." If God is present in you in all phases of growth, God must be here and now, too. See how God is in you right now.

BREAKING
THE COCOON
OF ISOLATION

WE HAVE created our own cocoons, "This is me, so-called Shantanand." What is this Shantanand? Is it a reality? We live in the same cosmos, we share the same air, light, and earth, yet we create boundaries for the sake of our ego. "This is me, and everyone should know how great I am" is an illusion of the ego. Through selfless love and sharing, we break this illusion that we are separate and great, or separate and rotten, and we realize that we are part of the one great whole.

———————————

IN THE IMAGE
OF
THE DIVINE

SO TAKE A LITTLE time for self-regulation, a little time and money for selfless service, and a lot of time for self-acceptance and self-celebration. When you go to the mirror, don't rush and comb your hair so that you will look well in the eyes of others. Take time and really look at your divinity: "My eyes are beautiful. I can see through these beautiful eyes. How God is shining through my eyes, through my lips. God makes graceful movements through my hands." Did you create yourself? You are His painting, Her painting. You are divine. If you appreciate yourself, you are appreciating the great Painter. Unless you see yourself in that light, your mind compares you with others and you feel either proud ("What is wrong with you?") or inadequate ("What is wrong with me?").

This conviction that there is something wrong is a great block. You love your children, you love your husband or wife, you love your dog, you love flowers and rainbows— but you don't love yourself. Why not? The divinity within you is changeless. Even though you've gotten drunk, been foolish, cheated, and been cheated, your inner divinity has remained the same. When you appreciate yourself, you are not building your ego; you are becoming impersonal to the personal self. When you learn to become impersonal to your personal self, you appreciate God's grace, God's light in you.

Accept yourself without going into past guilt or future fantasies, and celebrate the moment. Even if you don't feel great every moment, negative feelings don't last. If you feel badly about yourself because you once were lustful, are you still lustful now? Even if you try to hold onto lust, you cannot. Try holding onto greed: "I am greedy ... I am greedy ... I am greedy." Greed is a thought. Can any thought be constantly present in your consciousness? When you are greedy, you are not lustful. When you are lustful, you are not greedy. When there is one feeling, other feelings are missing. These feelings of lust, greed, jealousy, and insecurity are different outfits. Sometimes you wear this shirt, sometimes that one. Can you say that if you have no shirt, you are no longer there? If you continue to be, in spite of all these feelings, who are you?

Unless you can appreciate yourself for doing your best, you will not hit the mark, even if you have the best intentions and achieve your best. So do your best—but also appreciate yourself for it, and appreciate Divine Essence within you.

What can you, or I, do better right now? For example, I am addressing these words to you. If my intention is to share as best I can, then I am blessed to be able to share what I am sharing. I feel the utmost satisfaction that this is the best I can do. This is the greatest moment of my life, because any moment when I do my best is the greatest.

Can you sense the same feeling in you? You are here. Even if you don't like my words, you are courteous enough to keep reading. Appreciate your courteousness, and acknowledge how wonderful you are for not running away.

276

And if you are not enduring these words but enjoying them, feel good about that. Acknowledge how wonderful you are for listening and letting these words of peace, freedom, and joy permeate your being. There is really no block to attaining enlightenment except lack of faith in your own inherent purity and goodness. You doubt your own worth. When you don't doubt, you find it is there.

MAKE SPACE
FOR
DIVINE GRACE

MAKE SPACE for divine grace, make time for divine service, for chanting, for your focal point, for being yourself and celebrating yourself.

Find a group where you can be yourself, where people are not trying to change you and you are not trying to change others. In those groups where you don't feel threatened, you feel a sense of impersonal being; and the more you get in touch with that impersonal being, the more you get out of your self-consciousness, your limited consciousness. In the beginning, you need some feedback. If you have the feedback of the group, you develop confidence to pursue your spiritual quest on your own.

Chanting is a way of opening your heart to cosmic light, love, and joy and getting in touch with your divinity. You start by enjoying the melody and gradually get in touch with that space where you can just flow and be yourself. Some people may not be open to chanting, but it is one of the best means of relaxing and transcending self-consciousness. You don't have to chant names that are foreign to you; you may chant Jesus or Mary, you may chant about love, peace, and life. Create your own chants.

❦

ENLIGHTENMENT

YOU CANNOT experience enlightenment when you are fragmented. So decide what thought you want to entertain, and ignore the others. In the process of ignoring them, you will have a sense of self-victory and cheerfulness about your decisiveness.

Unless you become aware of your healing presence, you will not be able to heal yourself or the world. You have to be humble; but humility does not mean denying your Divine Essence. Enlightenment is nothing more than realizing this Essence.

You don't have to be scholarly, pure, disciplined, or meditative to recognize that you are yourself. Your body is constantly changing; your thoughts are constantly changing; yet somehow you are sure you are the same self. When you are in touch with this changeless Essence within you, you are enlightened.

Most of us have illusions about enlightenment, which we must first recognize and then get rid of. Enlightenment does not mean being blissed out and avoiding life's challenges. Enlightenment is what makes you strong enough to challenge your fears and to be truly yourself. When we think of Jesus, Buddha, or any great, enlightened person, we find them to be very human. They did not turn into holy statues and lose their human sensitivity. They continued to care about others. They shared their teachings and love with all mankind.

WHY COMPARTMENTALIZE GOD?

THERE IS NO deeper illusion than thinking we are spiritual. If you think, "Now I am spiritual, holy, and meditative," you are just feeding your ego. When you truly realize your Divine Essence of changelessness, then you become free of yourself. And when you become free of yourself, it will no longer feel good to confine yourself to your own body and mind.

Only those who feel suffocated by the self-centeredness of their lives can dare to be spiritual. Once you are fed up with ordinary pursuits, you won't have to seek divine bliss—it will seek you.

If you are not yet fed up, then recognize this and be honest, total, and courageous about it. Pursue ordinary things sincerely and wholeheartedly. If you cannot appreciate God as cosmic consciousness, then recognize God in the form of a beautiful person. When you find such a person, treat him or her with the utmost love and adoration, as if God had come into your life. God appears to us every moment, in just the way we are ready to appreciate. When we are open to receive God, a cup of tea is not simply a cup of tea, a person not simply a person, a rainbow not simply a rainbow. Instead, it is something awesome, a mystical experience, in which you become open and transcend your individuality.

Why do you want to compartmentalize God, as if God can be realized only through a mantra or a scripture or a guru? God can be realized that way, but God can also be realized here and now. Make yourself pay attention. You don't have to make water holy to have it flow toward the ocean. You don't have to do special rituals for flame to rise toward the sun. It is already happening. The sun shines on everyone without judging, "This is holy, that is unholy, this is good, that is bad."

If sunlight is all-accepting, all-embracing, what about the source of the sunshine, the Divine Essence? It has no power to say "no" to anyone. We all are sustained by that universal Essence. On this earth there are beautiful fruit trees and flowers, and there are many poisonous herbs. The soil embraces them all. This Divine Essence exists within each.

REACHING
THE
BOILING POINT

IF YOU PUT WATER on to boil for a cup of tea but turn off the heat every few seconds, the water will never boil. You have to keep the heat on for some time. Yet in your spiritual pursuits, you turn on and off, on and off. One moment you turn on and say, "God is everywhere, God is within me, I am divine." The next moment you turn off and say, "I have eaten too much, I have not done my exercise, I have not been faithful." When your mind wavers, it never reaches that boiling point of realizing the Divine Essence. Expose yourself wholly to that Divine Essence, and appreciate yourself for recognizing it within you. The more you appreciate yourself for recognizing this changeless Essence within you, the sooner you will realize its divine bliss.

SURRENDERING

ENLIGHTENMENT IS recognizing the flow of life and surrendering to it. Real surrender does not mean surrendering with your will power. As long as you use your will power to surrender, you don't know what surrendering is. You surrender to many things—to the night, to the day, to seasons, to aging. You accept by recognizing that you have no other choice. As long as you think you have a choice, you think you can choose to hold back or let go. When you realize that it is happening anyway, that you are helpless, you fall flat and realize you have fallen at the feet of the Divine.

Be available to yourself. Don't keep yourself so busy with money and relationships that you are suffocated by life. Allow yourself to be poor, unproductive, without a lover—but be available to yourself. When you are available to yourself, you create a magnetic force, and all the riches of the world automatically come toward you. But if you are divided within yourself, then no matter what you have or who loves you, you will find fault with them. That negativity will create blocks in the way of your enlightenment.

Be kind to yourself and to others. Congratulate yourself

when you handle a moment consciously and lovingly. In celebrating a moment, you will penetrate the moment and realize eternity. If you fail to celebrate the moment, you will miss eternity.

At this moment, I am peaceful with you. You are peaceful with me. I allow myself to be myself. You allow yourself to be yourself. For me it feels great. For you it feels great. I realize nothing has been added to me—I am the same self. You realize nothing has been added to you—you are the same self. I realize I am missing nothing. You realize you are missing nothing.

When we are missing nothing, although we have received nothing, we are enlightened.

———————————

Knowing
Your
DIVINITY

WE ARE DIVINE. Since we are already Divine, we don't have to do anything to become so. If we could be Divine by doing something or becoming something, our Divinity would not be Divine. It would be a fabrication of the ego's dream of manipulating and becoming.

You are Divine, but because you are unaware of your Divinity you are looking for it. Sometimes you are looking for your glasses and do not realize you are wearing them. As long as you think you have lost them you continue looking for them, but when somebody tells you they are on your nose, you feel happy. Whether we are spiritual or nonspiritual, each of us is looking for this Divinity. So never think in an egotistical way that because you are going to church or studying meditation, you are special or evolved.

As water runs toward the ocean, it is the nature of mind to run toward its Source of Divinity. The search for happiness and freedom is the search for your Divine Essence, and it will never be complete unless and until you realize that Essence. Each of us is looking for it according to our own tendencies, our own understanding, and the particular hangups of our own mind. One is on the path of knowledge;

another is on the path of action; another is on the path of meditation; another is on the path of devotion and love. There are many paths, and there is nothing wrong with any of them.

THE PATH OF KNOWLEDGE
AND
THE TWO SELVES

THE PATH OF knowledge is the most direct. It tells you that you are already there. It does not ask you to believe even in Divine Essence or God. It does not ask you to believe in your teacher. It asks you to believe in your own self. Not the mystical, universal Self—forget about that. Who knows whether the Self exists or not? Just believe in your own, mundane self. Hold onto whatever you feel you are in a practical and objective way, according to your own knowing and understanding. This path requires us to be real with ourselves—with our feelings, aspirations, ambitions, hangups, fears, insecurities, and securities. This path does not ask you to believe in anything that does not make sense to your own common sense. It does not suggest that you go anywhere or do anything. It demands from your side only that you accept yourself the way you are. This is very, very difficult.

Your mind says, "How can I accept myself when I am jealous, angry, compulsive, indecisive, and lazy? If I accept myself, I will remain complacent; I will not improve; I will never experience the purpose of life." You have to understand that unless you accept yourself, you will not be able to transcend yourself, and unless you transcend yourself, you will not be able to realize your real Self.

There are two selves involved here. One is the gross physical self through which I am talking or you are listening, and one is the higher Self. You will not be able to transcend your limited self unless you are in touch with that limited self and accept it. Unless you transcend this little, gross self, you will not realize your universal Self.

On this path, you are asked, "How can you convince yourself that you are all right?" You have no choice but to accept yourself, since you are the way you are. That you can do something and improve is a fiction that you have created in your mind. You do whatever you are led to do, and you are led to do whatever you are ready to do.

Suppose you create the fiction that you have to catch your shadow. You are very smart, you have a Ph.D. and special mystical powers, and you are running after your shadow. So far, you have not been successful, but you do not want to give up. How many times do you have to fail before you recognize that even if you are very wise or holy, you are not going to catch your shadow? The pain is very great because your investment has been so heavy in chasing your shadow that you don't want to admit it cannot be done. Similarly, your investment has been so heavy in your fictitious self that you aren't willing to give up on it.

A child was trying to catch his shadow, but whenever he moved forward, his shadow moved away. He began to cry. His father came to console him saying, "A shadow can never be caught, but if the object casting the shadow is caught, then the shadow is also caught." He placed the child's hand on his head, and the child began to laugh. He had caught his shadow.

This path is a little hard to understand. You have to use your head, and it is hard on the head. It is not much concerned with your heart. Your heart has to be willing to recognize the Truth, and that is the only contribution from your heart on this path. The major understanding will come from the head. On this path, if you understand the Truth clearly through your head, it will sink into your heart. It is not something you just rationalize; in time, you start feeling also.

A king's infant son was kidnapped. Twenty years later, a robber was caught, and through various investigations the king found out that the robber was his son. All the thoughts he originally had toward the robber turned into compassion. This was his own child, who, it turned out, had been kidnapped and not been raised in the right way, so he had turned into a robber. The recognition that the robber was his son transformed the king's feelings. When you realize the Truth, you feel love.

THE
CHALLENGE

IT IS THE NATURE of the mind to go through ups and downs. Sometimes it will be peaceful, sometimes aggravated, sometimes dull and sleepy. When you are a little more clear, you will see that all of this is okay. When the mind is absolutely clear, it is filled with love, it is entranced. That is called bliss. According to scriptures, "When a man of wisdom is in either a clear space of understanding, a restless space of achieving and proving, or a space of dullness and inertia, he accepts all three states of mind with ease and equanimity."

You are fighting with yourself. You think that your mind is the way it is because you are not enlightened; but even an enlightened person's mind goes through these three states of serenity, activity, or inertia. These states belong to the three gunas and operate through all of us. You are the same person, but you experience in three different ways according to those three energies. It is as normal as hunger, but you have not accepted it as normal.

WITHOUT A PROBLEM,
CAN YOU EXIST?

YOU HAVE YOUR own quota of serenity, but because you fight with restlessness and dullness, you lose awareness of serenity. Try to accept yourself for ten minutes and see what happens. When you really accept yourself, the problem you had fizzles out. It is your subjective involvement with and reaction to the problem that perpetuates, intensifies, and aggravates it.

The problem is that you will not feel happy without having a problem. You have felt useful sorting out the problem and fighting with it. The moment you find there is no problem, you feel useless, so you want to have a problem. When you find there is no problem, you start fizzling out too.

That is the final stage of transition. As a particular person, you can only exist in opposition to something. You can exist only if you have something to relate to. When you have nothing to interact with, you cannot survive as an individual self. That is the challenge on this Path of Knowledge.

In this transition, you will feel insecure. It is easy for you to conclude that you are insecure, lustful, or compulsive;

but on this path, instead of drawing conclusions you are asked to be available to yourself and see how long this insecurity, lustfulness, or compulsiveness lasts. To do that, you have to be available in that place. You cannot assume that because you left a dog in your house, the dog must be *in* the house. You have to be in the house and see the dog to verify that the dog is there. We all complain, "Nobody understands, nobody is faithful." Is this wild dog of compulsiveness, lustfulness, insecurity, and indecisiveness always faithfully there in your mind? Who will know for you if the dog is there or not?

You are praying to God, "God help me get rid of this dog, I am tired of this dog." What are you expecting from God? If you call and say, "Swamiji, I love you," I will feel pleased; but if you keep calling me, "Swamiji, I love you, I love you, I love you," I will say, "Get out. Leave me alone!" If you say to your mirror, "I love you, I love you, I love you," what can the mirror do for you? The mirror inspires you; your reflection inspires you; but you have to use your own hands to fix your makeup.

On this path, you are thrown back on yourself. On this path, whatever you do, you do directly. Nobody is going to do it for you. Here you see the contradiction: Although you are the non-doer, you take full responsibility. When you are hungry, God will not eat for you. When you need to go to the bathroom, God will not go to the bathroom for you. God is all-powerful, but He can only go to the bathroom for you *through* you. You have to love God, but don't expect too much from God. On this path, when you attend to yourself and become available to yourself, you find that the negative thoughts, desires, and tendencies fizzle out; and when they fizzle out, you find that "you" also fizzle out.

You want to sleep, but your partner is disturbing you. When your partner is gracious enough to not disturb you,

you fall asleep. When you have fallen asleep, where is the person who was fighting with your partner? When you fall asleep, you lose both the partner and that person who was complaining against the partner. In sound sleep, the one who was troubled by the restless partner is no longer there. It has merged into sleep.

Because of this crazy mind, I experience "Shantanand." When the mind falls asleep, Shantanand is merged into that sleep. Your individual self that has all the problems will be gone when you stop playing with the thoughts. You are ready for whatever you are ready for. If you are not ready, it is all right not to be ready. You want to be ready as you are. So you are not as great as Mother Teresa. Be willing to accept yourself as you are.

When I was a boy, the older boys used to talk about girls, and I wondered why. They told me, "One day when you are older, you will understand why we talk about girls." I wondered, "Can't I understand now?" It used to bother me when they said I had to be older to understand. I felt hurt that they did not give validity to my intelligence. Later on, I realized they were right. I tried my best but could not understand any earlier. When the right time came, I understood without asking anyone. It was okay not understanding at that time. It's okay if you don't feel a burning zeal for self-realization, God-realization, or selfless service. It all comes in the process of growth.

Your Nature
Is
Fullness

SEE HOW HAPPY children are, smiling and laughing, radiating so much energy and bliss. With all our wisdom and understanding, we rarely exude such bliss. Children experience fullness. Some adults, those who are more advanced, experience the same fullness.

Fullness is interpreted in different ways. Fullness is universal, fullness is Divine, and you are made of that fullness. The moment you accept yourself with all your limitations, you are celebrating your fullness; and when you celebrate your fullness, you forget about your limitations. When you trust yourself, when you accept yourself, when you are available to yourself, you will realize that "you" are missing; God is shining.

Look into yourself and see how long you can maintain objective awareness of what you find. Don't get involved subjectively with, "Here is my insecurity, my desire, my compulsiveness, my indecisiveness, my search for God." The search for God is also a thought. Seeking is a fabrication of the mind. When you fall asleep, do you seek anything? Seeking is not your real nature. Your real nature is fullness. When you get in touch with yourself, you will find you don't really need to seek. When there is no seeking, there is no seeker, only fullness. Just be yourself. Accept your thoughts of rottenness, insecurity, fear, or jealousy, and they will be transformed into Divinity. If you don't give validity to the thoughts, they fizzle out like a wave sinking back into the ocean.

On this path, you are supposed to challenge your teacher, and if your teacher is really loving and open, he will be happy that you are being a good student by challenging him. If you take things for granted, you don't belong on this Path of Knowledge because you are not inclined toward challenges; your mind is too dull. Don't accept anything; don't believe anything unless it makes sense to you. If something does not make sense, don't believe it. Keep your questions for five minutes. After five minutes, see if your question stays in your heart.

GUIDED
MEDITATION

HOW DO YOU feel? ... Observe your feelings ... If you feel great, celebrate the feeling ... If you feel bad, accept that too ... Pin down what makes you feel bad ... Accept whatever you find and observe how long that cause stays in the space of your consciousness ... Every cause that makes you feel bad right now is a thought, and every thought by nature is fleeting ... When this particular thought disappears, you cannot feel bad anymore ...

You are just being yourself now ... If you find it easier, you may keep your eyes open ... If you are alert, you will find that bliss that you have been seeking ... That surge of love will overwhelm your being ... That surge of peace will absorb your individual self ...

Do you have a problem, or are you enjoying problem-lessness?

... You are either fearless or facing your fear ... You are either content or facing your discontent ... Clarity is the key on this Path of Knowledge ... Be clear ...

Don't imagine anything ... Hang loose and be clear ... Even if you feel bored, accept boredom ... See how long boredom stays in the space of your consciousness ... Nothing can hurt you; you can only fall asleep in this boredom, so fall asleep ... Accept yourself ... Get in touch with yourself and see if you really care for God or enlightenment ... If you don't care, don't feel bad that you don't care ... Just be yourself ... God will wait for you ... He wants to see you happy ... Either you are happy or unhappy ... If you are unhappy, pin down the cause of your unhappiness and see how long it stays in the space of your consciousness ... If you are happy, just enjoy yourself ...

Be alert and watch how one thought is replaced by another, how one desire is replaced by another, how one feeling is replaced by another ... You are not doing anything to replace them ... It just happens on its own ... You simply observe it ... You cannot observe unless you are there, unless you are available.

Now, for two minutes we will do an experiment with a fast, deep breathing exercise. Breathing is closely related to the mind, and it is the mind that thinks it is bound and has to find God. When you temporarily suspend your breathing, your thoughts also go through a temporary state of suspension, and you get a glimpse of freedom.

To reach that state, you will do ten very deep breaths. Then increase the speed of the breaths and make them very fast. Within a minute, you will feel exhausted, so you will stop breathing; but before you stop breathing, inhale as much as you can and retain the air inside. Remember to stop the breathing only after the inhalation and do not exhale.

While you are holding the air, just watch how your mind feels. You will find that your mind is free of all thoughts, desires, and emotions, and you are feeling great. Then gradually you will release the air in a gentle way.

First, start breathing very deeply many times ... Now faster, let your whole body bounce up and down as though you are riding a horse ... faster, faster, deeper, deeper ... Now, INHALE AND STOP.

How do you feel? Get in touch with your feeling, get in touch with your space ... You are in touch with your is-ness, your pure existence, free of all thoughts, desires, emotions, and conditionings.

... You are you, content within yourself ... You are in touch with your Divine Essence, which is content by nature.

When you are at peace with yourself, you accept yourself the way you are. You accept your body, you accept your mind. Divine Essence is within you and outside. Relax yourself and be yourself. Relax as if you were absolutely alone; others are simply statues. How would you like to be if you were all alone here?

Now you can open your eyes and look around. Everything is just a mirror. Just look at things as though you are going to read your reflection in them.

When you see different forms, you compare yourself with others and find fault. When you realize your universal Self, you realize it is you as Mother Teresa through Mother Teresa; it is you as Shantanand through Shantanand; it is you as Bill through Bill. Water has no special form of its own; it takes the form of its container. The Divine Essence in you and in me is like water. Each form is expressing that Essence as a particular person.

The body is the container, and the Spirit is the water. Between the two comes the mind like a ripple and thinks, "This container is better than that." The container has no problem, the water has no problem; the ripple has the problem. If the ripple could realize it is made of water and it is all the same water, it would accept any container.

You may not be the sun, but you will accept yourself as being a candle because you are needed as a candle. When two lovers are having supper, they don't want sunshine, they want candlelight to make it more romantic. You are the candlelight, and you are the sun.

SWAMI
SHANTANAND SARASWATI

SWAMI SHANTANAND Saraswati was born in North India in 1946. He graduated with Honors from the University of Allahabad, India. He came to the United States in 1980.

As a young man, Shantanand was contemplative about the mysteries of life. He was inspired by the lives of Buddha, Jesus, Ramakrishna Paramahansa and Ramana Maharshi, and was deeply influenced by his guru, Vishnudevananda Saraswati.

Following his teacher's instructions, Shantanand spent several years living in a cave practicing Raja Yoga and meditation. There, he realized he should follow and teach Jnana Yoga, the path of knowledge and understanding. This path emphasizes self-inquiry and self-observation and leads one to an understanding of the mind and how to transcend the duality of what we see versus what is real. Shantanand translates ancient Vedantic wisdom into modern psychology, beyond religion, tradition, and customs.

301

He says, "You know you are you, not because of your body, thoughts and feelings which are constantly changing, but because of the Divine Essence within you, which is changeless."

He has established two centers in North India as well as Shanti Temple in New York. He has written several books, lectured throughout the United States, and appeared on numerous radio and television programs. He is available for private counseling, lectures and retreats. He can be reached at: Shanti Temple, 43 South Main Street, Spring Valley, NY 10977; (914) 356-8104.

INDEX

307

310

311

ORDER FORM

To order contact:
National Book Network
4720 Boston Way
Lanham, MD 20706
1 (800) 462-6420
Visa and Master Card accepted

Pure Wisdom: Insights for those Seeking Happiness and Peace of Mind. $10.95.

The Spiritual Seeker's Guide: The Complete Source for Religions and Spiritual Groups of the World. $12.95.

Straight from the Heart: Authors, Celebrities and Others Share Their Philosophies on Making a Difference in the World. $10.95.